GENERATION

Les Lawrence

Elisha Vision Publishing

> *Who has ascended into heaven, or descended? Who has gathered the wind in His fists? Who has bound the waters in a garment? Who has established all the ends of the earth? What is His name, and what is His Son's name, If you know?* Proverbs 30:4

Cover Graphics by Dean Schuster of truematter.com.

This book is available through:

Elisha Vision Publishing

P.O. Box 1601

Wake Forest, NC 27588

Or it can be ordered directly from www.ElishaVision.com

This book was printed in the USA by

InstantPublisher.com
P.O. Box 340, 410 Highway 72 W.
Collierville TN 38027

ISBN 978-0-9843958-0-4

DEDICATION

This book is dedicated to the memory and inspiration of Pastor Earl Waterman of Dalton Mtn., New Hampshire, who was nearly 100 years old when he passed in July of 2009. He often said "I am not a prophet or a prophet's son, but I'll do the prophesying till the prophet comes!" He is the one who charged me in 1985 saying:

"Prophesy, young man, prophesy!"

ACKNOWLEDGMENTS

First, my gratitude goes to my Messiah Yeshua, the Lord Jesus, Whom I have come to know as Yeshua ben YAHWEH, Jesus, Son of God! The love of my life, my beautiful wife, Doreen, is my best friend and my greatest help.

I thank my brother and personal pastor, Ken Lawrence, and his wife of 50 years, Mavis, of River of Life Church in Sandpoint, Idaho, for their love and oversight through many years. There is also a special place in my heart for John & Sara Jean Fisk. Thank you, John, for our symbiotic relationship that always leads us to that "third opinion" in discovering truth together. My newest friend and brother, Dwayne Parsons, has been a practical help in marketing, inspiring me to enlarge my vision. Much honor is due to a true example of the faith, my dearly loved brother, Arthur Burt of Wales, a man of a great God.

I also want to thank my dear personal friends: Dick & Anna May Hoffman, Dave & Sandy Campbell, LaVonne Summer, Rob & Ruth Brown, Sirus & Kaye Chitsaz, Bill & Gloria Morgan, Bruce & Viki Johnson, Janssen & Amy Carr-Barfield and Doug & Leslie Walton; for their encouragement and understanding of my heart for Israel and my "Elisha Vision".

Finally, great appreciation also goes to the congregation at Shalom Peniel and the Issachar Forum, my outstanding Bible Class at Covenant Church International, our faithful house church, and the brothers in my Friday morning accountability group for all their prayers and encouragement.

Contents

Introduction

We are living the final chapters of history. This book is about timing. I believe we are living in the last generation before the millennium. What should we be doing? What is coming next? Is it all gloom and doom? No! I like to say, it is not gloom and doom, but gloom and va-voom!

There is an excitement to this day. It has been reported that, in 1922, Smith Wigglesworth emphasized that what he carried in God was not to be envied, but instead, he envied what the last generation will see. This is it! I do not emphasize escape, but our empowerment to function. Daniel spoke of our day in chapter 11:32: *the people who know their God shall be strong, and carry out great exploits.* Even though Jesus will come as a thief in the night, He will not surprise us as a thief, because we are not of the night, but of the day. His mysteries have been revealed to those who know His voice.

There is no attempt here to defend every action of Israel's present government. The focus is the prophetic purpose of the God of Abraham, Isaac and Jacob. God will accomplish His eternal purpose, either with us or without us. Nowhere is this more evident than in the issue of modern Israel. The controversy surrounding the Middle East will not diminish; it is destined to expand.

Red Sea Sunrise

Turquoise water -- tan sand -- and a tangerine sun! It was without question one of the most beautiful and indescribable sights of my 45 years. Words fail to adequately portray the splendor on that exquisite shore of the timeless Red Sea. My friend, Duane Trochessett, and I had just come from Jerusalem in January 1990. We had participated in the most powerful prayer conference we had ever attended. After speaking to a congregation in Tiberias on Shabbat, Israel's Sabbath, we traversed Israel from Galilee in the North, to the southernmost Israeli seaport of Eilat. This modern city is located at the northern tip of the Red Sea. From there, we endured a rickety Egyptian public bus ride five hours further south through the Sinai Peninsula to a spot near its southernmost point. We lugged a two-man tent with us, which we pitched on a deserted stretch of Red Sea beach, a few miles north of Sharm el Sheikh, Egypt.

We heard that the Red Sea had some of the most beautiful coral reefs in the world along these shores and we were not disappointed. We walked up the pristine beach two or three miles, seeing no one else and feeling alone in the world. We then drifted and snorkeled, swimming with the current back to our tent location among picturesque rocks on the tan beach. That the Red Sea had such underwater beauty had never occurred to me before. I am a native son of Prophetstown, Illinois among the cornfields of the Midwestern prairie. Swimming in the midst of such an indescribable spectacle of tropical fish of every variety was a shock. The Bible does not refer to it, except for Pharaoh's chariots and army ending up there.

Our greatest sight occurred the next morning at first light. The setting was already surreal; just being in such an exotic location at a time of personal renewal with God. We opened the flap on our eastward facing tent and were stunned with the view. Rising out of the turquoise sea was the largest sun we had ever seen, almost close enough to touch. It was the most incredible shade of color; the closest I can come is tangerine! It was perfectly round as it rose on the horizon, resurrecting out of the water. The lack of pollution in the cloudless blue sky eliminated the sun's rays, making the stark contrast more amazing between that brilliant reddish-orange sun, the blue sky and the turquoise sea. The only slight comparison I can make is to the occasional beautiful orange harvest moon I have seen a few times in New England. But this was the sun, a thousand times deeper in that surreal tangerine color, and a million times more radiant! Duane and I worshipped the Creator on that beach in a depth of personal connection with Him unlike any previous experience. We were not worshipping the creation, but the One Who had created. As you read this book, please try to rise above the history and logic of the words to see the God of the Bible Who is the Faithful God of history.

The Rise of Israel

Modern Israel has risen out of the sea of nations like that tangerine sun. In my opinion, this may be the most important book written on the subject of Israel and the Mid-East in this decade because of the critical message it contains for Christians. The amazing reappearance of Israel as a nation has profound importance regarding the nature of God. He directly links His covenant with Israel to His faithful nature as seen in all creation:

> *Thus says YAHWEH, Who gives the sun for a light by day, The ordinances of the moon and the stars for a light by night, Who disturbs the sea, And its waves roar (YAHWEH of hosts is His name): "If those ordinances depart From before Me, says YAHWEH, Then the seed of Israel shall also cease From being a nation before Me forever"* (Jer. 31:36).

The nature of God's faithfulness, as a theological tenet, is being seriously undermined by Western Christian "pop theology" that divorces Christianity from its Jewish roots. But even more seriously, it *divorces God from His own character.* If God lied or changed His mind about His unconditional promises to Israel, then there would be no basis left to believe His covenant to Christians. God is either a covenant keeper or a covenant breaker. It cannot be both ways.

> *Hear the word of YAHWEH, O nations, And declare it in the isles afar off, and say, "He who*

scattered Israel will gather him, And keep him as a shepherd does his flock." (Jer. 31:10).

You shall no longer be termed Forsaken, Nor shall your land any more be termed Desolate; But you shall be called Hephzibah, and your land Beulah; For YAHWEH delights in you, And your land shall be married. (Is. 62:4).

The Faithful God

The theme of this book is the faithfulness of God. The Creator has revealed Himself in many ways. He is the only true God and can be seen in all He has created. He is also revealed in the written word...the Holy Scriptures. Among all the ways of revelation however, there remains a particularly clear unveiling of the faithful God. He is revealed in His relationship with one land and one specific people: Israel, His sign to the whole world.

This is not to deny His loving relationship with all peoples who will seek Him. All of God's activities in the entire earth are *derived* from the critical fact of His own character: *faithfulness!* Thus, how God views Israel over the course of history, shows the standard of integrity issuing directly from His own character. This is of utmost importance, first to the people of Israel and then to all the other nations that are destined to be included. The biblical analogy is of one plant with branches broken off, wild branches grafted into the original plant, and finally some of the broken off branches being grafted back into the *same* planting.

Even the scripture record itself, with the great promise of salvation through the Messiah Yeshua (Jesus) and all the other Bible promises, *does not stand alone!* The veracity or truthfulness of the written word is only as sure as the truthful character of the author. The source of the Bible's authority is the Person of YAHWEH who reveals Himself through the awesome process of many writers over many centuries of time. But if God lies or breaks His word in any way, then the *basis of believing* is lost. The word of a liar is worthless. But God only speaks truth, because *God is truth!*

God's *power* is manifested in creation but His *faithful nature* is particularly confirmed in Israel. As surely as that tangerine sun rose over the Red Sea, God is raising up Israel out of the sea of nations in prophetic fulfillment of His eternal purpose.

GOD IS FAITHFUL!

Chapter 1

The Generation LAST

Scoffers will come in the last days, walking according to their own lusts, and saying, "Where is the promise of His coming? For since the fathers fell asleep, all things continue as they were from the beginning of creation" (2 Peter 3:3-4).

It is very hard for most people, even Christians, to believe that this is the last generation before the end of the age. So much history has passed. So many generations before have believed theirs was the last, and yet they were wrong. However, there is a generation that will be right to make that claim. This book offers my evidence that we are living in the last generation.

Two Proofs

There are two clear proofs in Biblical prophecy that we are now living in the last generation. One is Psalm 102, which I call the Holocaust Psalm. The second proof is in Jesus' own words. It is found in the Olivet discourse, recorded in Matthew 24, Mark 13 and Luke 21.

Look into the rear view mirror of history for the key that unlocks both of these revelations. Many missed Jesus in His first coming by misreading prophecy, and the same happens today. However, once you have seen the historical fulfillment it becomes clear. Both the Old and New Testament scriptures offered here are directly tied to recent events that are now history and cannot be refuted. They both refer to literal fulfillment of events in modern Israel that prove we are in the last generation. Psalm 102 has a hidden truth that identifies this very generation as *the last*.

The Holocaust

The Holocaust is the term generally used to describe the genocide of approximately six million European Jews during World War II, a program of systematic state-sponsored extermination by Nazi Germany, under Adolf Hitler, its allies, and collaborators.

Some scholars maintain that the definition of the Holocaust should also include the Nazis' systematic murder of millions of people in other groups, including Catholics, ethnic Poles, the Romani, Soviet civilians, Soviet prisoners of war, people with disabilities, homosexuals, Jehovah's Witnesses, and other political and religious opponents. By this definition, the total number of Holocaust victims would be between 11 million and 17 million people. Quote from Wikipedia (en.wikipedia.org/wiki/The_Holocaust)

The Holocaust evokes primal visceral responses to all confronted by such palpable evil. The Jews curse and remember, the culpable world minimizes and forgets, and anti-Semites deny it ever happened. Thus the events of the Holocaust are challenged, cloaked and denied through political correctness and revisionist history. Yet, these events leap from the pages of the prophetic Word of God.

Psalm 102 – The Holocaust Psalm

Most people do not think of the Psalms as prophecy, yet the Psalms do factually foretell events being fulfilled at this time in history. Psalms 2 and 83 are good examples, but Psalm 102 in particular, has much to offer the student of end time prophecy. The Holocaust is poignantly apparent in the first eleven verses. They are quoted in full, so that you may absorb the emotional impact as you read. Please contemplate every word as you meditate.

(A Prayer of the afflicted, when he is overwhelmed and pours out his complaint before YAHWEH.) *Hear my prayer, YAHWEH, And let my cry come to You. Do not hide Your face from me in the day of my trouble; Incline Your ear to me; In the day that I call, answer me speedily. For my days are consumed like smoke, And my bones are burned like a hearth. My heart is stricken and withered like grass, So that I forget to eat my bread. Because of the sound of my groaning My bones cling to my skin. I am like a pelican of the wilderness; I am like an owl of the desert. I lie awake, And am like a sparrow alone on the housetop. My enemies reproach me all day long; Those who deride me swear an oath against me. For I have eaten ashes like bread, And mingled my drink with weeping, Because of Your indignation and Your wrath; For You have lifted me up and cast me away. My days are like a shadow that lengthens, And I wither away like grass.* (Psalm 102:1-11).

When you realize the actual Holocaust is described in these verses, you will never see this Psalm the same again. That is what happened to me; it is such an amazingly accurate and graphic description. God had this Psalm placed in Scripture 3,000 years ago for this very time of history. Now that you see it, let's see why God revealed it to us now. Verse three speaks of bones scorched in a hearth. Verse eight tells of using their names as a curse (Prison camp guards cursed them and required the yellow Star of David, with the name "Jew," on their clothing as a badge of contempt). Verse nine speaks of eating ashes like bread. Ashes of the burned bodies of family members were spewed from the concentration camps' crematoriums. Jewish ashes literally fell back on the camp defiling their food. The images keep coming: smoke, bones, burned, hearth, stricken, withered, grass, forget, groaning, cling, skin, awake, alone, enemies, reproach, deride, swear, ashes, weeping, indignation, wrath, cast away.

Can this possibly refer to any other event of history than the Holocaust? Yet, the Psalm does not end at verse eleven.

This prophetic Psalm abruptly turns on verse twelve, as the psalmist turns to YAHWEH out of the horrors of his vision, and perhaps personal experience of desperation. He sees the end of the matter. The Lord shall endure!

But You, O YAHWEH, shall endure forever, And the remembrance of Your name to all generations.

And then the psalmist sees the revelation of the purpose of God in verse thirteen:

You will arise and have mercy on Zion; For the time to favor her, Yes the set time, has come.

Set Time!

What a concept! God has a set, specific time to favor Zion. It is not that He caused the massacre of six million Jews, but seeing the end from the beginning, God marked that horrible event as the exact time to return favor to Zion. The Apostle Paul prophesied to our generation as the time of Israel's restoration and mercy:

*For if their being cast away is the reconciling of the world, what will their acceptance be but **life from the dead**?* (Romans 11:15).

Miraculously, within three years of the Holocaust, Israel was reborn as a nation in their historic land. First by the thousands and then by millions, Jews have returned to Israel from the four corners of the earth. Only God could have done it. Every other fallen nation or empire is gone forever, but Israel came back. The nation of Israel, scattered for 1,800 years, has been raised from the dead. Israel's resurrection is a testimony to Jesus, who said: *I am the resurrection and the life. He who believes in Me, though he may die, he shall live* (John 11:25). Jesus not only defeated death for Himself and the Church, but also for national Israel.

Disclaimer:

I do not believe dual covenant theology which says national Israel will be saved simply because they are Jews. They will be saved through the blood of Jesus, as He categorically declares none can come to the Father except through Him.

> *And I will pour on the house of David and on the inhabitants of Jerusalem the Spirit of grace and supplication; then they will look on Me whom they pierced.* (Zechariah 12:10)

> *For I do not desire, brethren, that you should be ignorant of this mystery, lest you should be wise in your own opinion, that blindness in part has happened to Israel until the fullness of the Gentiles has come in* (Romans 11:25).

Jewish salvation comes in God's promise to remove the scales from their eyes, to see that indeed Yeshua is Messiah. For nearly 2,000 years, they have been at a disadvantage when the Gospel is preached. But now, they are on level ground with everyone else to consider the claims of Jesus, that He is the Messiah of Israel and the son of God, Yeshua ben YAHWEH.

Hidden Revelation

We now come to the best part of Psalm 102. There is an amazing clue hidden here. God loves to hide things for us to discover. Proverbs 25:2 states: *It is the glory of God to conceal a matter, But the glory of kings is to search out a matter.* Jesus spoke in parables so that people would not understand truth without faith.

So what is the hidden gem? It is in verse eighteen: *This will be written for the generation to come, That a people yet to be created may praise YAHWEH.* Most English translations use a very general phrase at the end of the verse. Usually, it is something like: "for the generation to come" or "for a future generation." I recently spoke in a Brazilian church on Martha's Vineyard and noted that even in Portuguese it said "generacion futura." So, what is wrong with those translations? They all change the literal Hebrew from a very specific meaning, to a rather open general meaning. The literal Hebrew of this phrase means the **generation last**. The Hebrew word is "*acharown*" and it appears 51 times in the Hebrew Scriptures. Here is the list of how it is translated in the King James Bible with the number of times for each word: [last 20, after(ward)(s) 15, latter 6, end 2, utmost 2, following 1, hinder 1, hindermost 1, hindmost 1, rereward 1, uttermost 1] Can you tell me why translators used "future" or "to come" in Psalm 102:18? My theory is that God hid it so we could discover it in the actual last generation.

My conclusion for Psalm 102 is simple. It is a prophecy of the Holocaust. It describes the awful horror vividly, but then foretells God's redemptive plan for His "set time" to favor Zion with the rebirth of Israel. He then nails the prophecy down with the notation that this text and these events are particularly for the last generation. Therefore, I offer this Psalm as a proof that we are living in the terminal generation, the end of the age as we know it. I don't know exactly how long a generation is, but I definitely believe we are in it!

GOD IS FAITHFUL!

Chapter 2

Jesus Identifies Last Generation

We now turn to the Olivet Discourse to consider the second proof for the last generation, directly from the mouth of Jesus. How wonderful it would have been to sit at Jesus' feet during His earthly ministry. Yet, would we have understood any more than His disciples did? However, I believe that every single one of the Old and New Testament heroes of the faith would be absolutely thrilled to live in our day. This is the day they all longed to see! Just think of it. If this really is the last generation, many awesome events will transpire before our eyes.

One of the most preached passages in the Bible is found in Matthew 24. This is where we start looking for the second proof. Do you think of Jesus as a prophet? Yes, he was the greatest of all. Jesus starts by prophesying the destruction of the Temple which will leave not one stone on another. This prophecy of the fall of Jerusalem is our first clue. Jerusalem is set before the world as the key to the timing of the Second Coming.

Remember what devout Simeon had said while holding baby Jesus in his arms some thirty years earlier:

> *Behold, this Child is destined for the fall and rising of many in Israel, and for a sign which will be spoken against (yes, a sword will pierce through your own soul also), that the thoughts of many hearts may be revealed* (Luke 2:34-35).

Simeon prophesied that Jesus would preside over the fall and the rise of Israel. Jesus saw the beginning of the fall of Israel in his first advent, culminating with the fall of Jerusalem in 70AD, and will take command of a risen and saved Israel when He returns. So, the demise of Jerusalem and its restoration hold the key to understanding the signs of His coming.

The disciples asked Him directly: *Tell us, when will these things be? What will be the sign of Your coming and of the end of the age?* (Matthew 24:3). There is a hint in the fact that "sign" is singular. There are many signs of the end of the age, but only one sign of His coming. That sign is Jerusalem. It is the item in all three Gospels that is tied into historical timing. I will explain how later in this chapter. First, though, let's look at the end of the age.

> *And Jesus answered and said to them: "Take heed that no one deceives you. For many will come in My name, saying, 'I am the Christ,' and will deceive many. And you will hear of wars and rumors of wars. See that you are not troubled; for all these things must come to pass, but the*

end is not yet. For nation will rise against nation, and kingdom against kingdom. And there will be famines, pestilences, and earthquakes in various places. All these are the beginning of sorrows (Matthew 24:4-8).

There are general signs that happen throughout history but do not signal the end. But, in verse seven He gets more specific. The apparent repetition implied by "nation against nation" and "kingdom against kingdom" seems redundant. Both phrases appear to be talking about countries. But, then I discovered that in the Greek text, the first phrase was not nations, but "ethnos against ethnos". This is confirmed by recent history. There has been a major trend not just of countries fighting, but ethnic groups fighting each other within countries. A classic example of this is the Communist methodology of fomenting division between ethnic minorities and the dominant majority. This method is now being repeated by Islam. This is an indication that we are nearing the end.

Untimed Signs

The next warnings are of famines, pestilences, and earthquakes. These have increased exponentially in recent years accompanied by increased death and devastation. One example is the 2004 tsunami that killed over 220,000 people in the Indonesian area. Verse eight is even more specific when you look at the Greek words. "*The beginning of sorrows*" in the Greek is: "arche odin" which means: "the beginning of the pain of childbirth, travail pain, birth pangs". These birth pangs have already begun with the 20th Century world wars and depression. There are three characteristics of birth contractions. Once they start in earnest, there is no stopping them, the baby is coming. Second, they accelerate, increasing in intensity. Third, the contractions come closer together and last longer. If you look at the history of the last 100 years, you could make the case that we are well into the contractions. We have come too far to reverse it. We are about to see the birth of the Kingdom age and the reign of King Jesus!

People often ask me if I think it is going to get better and better or is it going to get worse and worse? My answer is a clear: "Yes, both!" It is going to get better for believers and worse for the world. Yet, getting better for believers, does not mean they will have no problems. It means God will give them glorious victories in the midst of trials and tribulations. Look at China and the Islamic countries and other places where the torture and death of believers is ongoing. But the Chinese underground church reveals amazing testimonies of believers. They actually pray that they would be found worthy to be arrested and suffer for Jesus. I know we in the West don't understand that part yet, but we will. How could Stephen, in the book of Acts, pray for his murderers as he was being stoned to death? Daniel escaped the lions' den, and the three thrown into the furnace come out unscathed. These are examples of God's protection and deliverance. As the three young men said:

*Our God whom we serve is **able to deliver us** from the burning fiery furnace, and He will deliver us from your hand, O king. **But if not**, let it be known to you, O king, that we do not serve your gods, nor will we worship the gold image which you have set up* (Daniel 3:17-18).

So, we rejoice in YAHWEH, if we live or if we die. We are in the arms of Jesus! We really do believe this is how it will be. Foxes Book of Martyrs repeats this testimony over and over again. We say with Paul: *For to me, to live is Christ, and to die is gain* (Philippians 1:21).

Timing Words

Now, let's follow the timing clue, Jerusalem. We have seen that Jesus prophesied the fall of Jerusalem which happened 35 or so years later. But He also prophesied the restoration of Jerusalem. How? You may ask. Let me explain from Luke's Gospel. Luke 21 through verse eleven lists similar sayings of Jesus (as Matthew and Mark's version). But, Luke introduces new details into the narrative. He steps back in verse twelve to the time before Jerusalem falls. Jesus says:

But before all these things, they will lay their hands on you and persecute you, delivering you up to the synagogues and prisons. You will be brought before kings and rulers for My name's sake. But it will turn out for you as an occasion for testimony. Therefore settle it in your hearts not to meditate beforehand on what you will answer; for I will give you a mouth and wisdom which all your adversaries will not be able to contradict or resist. You will be betrayed even by parents and brothers, relatives and friends; and they will put some of you to death. And you will be hated by all for My name's sake. But not a hair of your head shall be lost. By your patience possess your souls. But when you see Jerusalem surrounded by armies, then know that its desolation is near (Luke 21:12-20).

You can now see that the above passage is a description of the actual events that led up to the destruction of Jerusalem. Remember that we can hold the rear view mirror of history up to the prophecy and observe events as they actually happened. The next four verses are often placed in our future, but I maintain that they also were events before Jerusalem fell.

Then let those who are in Judea flee to the mountains, let those who are in the midst of her depart, and let not those who are in the country enter her. For these are the days of vengeance, that all things which are written may be fulfilled. But woe to those who are pregnant and to those who are nursing babies in those days! For there will be great distress in the land and wrath upon this people (Luke 21:21-23).

Gentile Rule of Jerusalem

The next verse is critical to see the point I am making. Historically, we come now to the fall of Jerusalem and the scattering of the Jews to all nations.

This is known by historians as the Diaspora, which simply means the dispersion:

> *And they will fall by the edge of the sword, and be led away captive into all nations. And Jerusalem will be trampled by Gentiles until the times of the Gentiles are fulfilled.* (Luke 21:24).

The intriguing part is the last half. What did Jesus mean by *trampled by Gentiles until the times of the Gentiles are fulfilled?* He was prophesying that the city would be under the dominion and control of Gentiles until their time to rule the city was fulfilled or finished. History confirms Gentile rule continued till this generation.

Remember that our study of Psalm 102 pointed to the last generation through the timing of the Holocaust and the miracle rebirth of national Israel. But Jerusalem did not come under Israel's control in 1948. Not until early June of 1967, during the Six Day War, could it be said that Jerusalem was no longer ruled by Gentiles. My wife, Doreen, and I have always had a sense of destiny connected to that amazing week because 6-11-67 was our wedding day.

The next eight verses describe physical signs that will precede **the sign**. Again, these multiple signs will occur, but are not time specific. The only historical single timing sign in Matthew, Mark and Luke is the restoration of Jerusalem to the sovereign control of Israel, after millennia of Gentile rule.

And there will be signs in the sun, in the moon, and in the stars; and on the earth distress of nations, with perplexity, the sea and the waves roaring; men's hearts failing them from fear and the expectation of those things which are coming on the earth, for the powers of the heavens will be shaken. Then they will see the Son of Man coming in a cloud with power and great glory. Now when these things begin to happen, look up and lift up your heads, because your redemption draws near. Then He spoke to them a parable: "Look at the fig tree, and all the trees. When they are already budding, you see and know for yourselves that summer is now near. So you also, when you see these things happening, know that the kingdom of God is near. **Assuredly, I say to you, this generation will by no means pass away till all things take place.** (Luke 21:32).

Jesus clearly states that there will be a generation that will not pass away till He comes. One thing it tells us is that mankind will not destroy the earth. There will be a last generation. The next question is simple. To which generation was He referring? It was obviously not the disciples, they died. Of course, it was not any other generation since then, because Jesus has not yet come. His analogy of the fig tree and all trees budding simply means that seeing buds on trees means summer is around the corner. Therefore Jesus was indicating that all of these signs occurring mean His return is near.

In summary, we have seen that the only historically time significant words in Matthew 24 and Luke 21 refer to Jerusalem under Israeli control coupled with His return. Is there any other logical conclusion Jesus could possibly have meant? The generation that sees the restoration of Jerusalem to Israeli sovereignty will not pass away till He comes! We are living in that generation, the **GENERATION LAST**.

GOD IS FAITHFUL!

Chapter 3

The Great Coming Merger

Let's take this one more step and consider what this means for the Church's relationship to Israel. From our study of Psalm 102 we learned that God favored Zion after the Holocaust. Jeremiah asked: Can a nation be born in a day? Israel was born in one day by vote of the United Nations on May 14, 1948. In addition, we see that Jerusalem is back in the hands of Israel since June 1967, fulfilling Luke 21.

For most of my 40+ years of preaching, I declared that Israel and the Church were on parallel tracks. A few years ago, however, the Lord corrected me. He showed me that they indeed are on separate tracks, but they are not parallel, they are merging! I have seen the revelation of one new man. Jews who believe in Jesus and former Gentiles, who believe in Jesus, will be joined together. The reason I say "former" Gentiles is because Paul speaks of the Ephesians and Corinthians, as Gentiles in the past tense since they accepted the Jewish Messiah.

*Therefore remember that you, once Gentiles in the flesh--who are called Uncircumcision by what is called the Circumcision made in the flesh by hands--that at that time you were without Christ, being aliens from the commonwealth of Israel and strangers from the covenants of promise, having no hope and without God in the world. But now in Christ Jesus you who once were far off have been brought near by the blood of Christ. For He Himself is our peace, who has made both one, and has broken down the middle wall of separation, having abolished in His flesh the enmity, that is, the law of commandments contained in ordinances, so as to create in Himself **one new man** from the two, thus making peace, and that He might reconcile them both to God in one body through the cross, thereby putting to death the enmity. And He came and preached peace to you who were afar off and to those who were near. For through Him we both have access by one Spirit to the Father. Now, therefore, you are no longer strangers and foreigners, but fellow citizens with the saints and members of the household of God* (Ephesians 2:11-19).

This last verse about the saints and the household of God refers to the Old Testament saints of Israel.

Greatest Revival

The greatest revival of history is destined to occur in the last generation. When Peter identified Pentecost in Acts 2 as the fulfillment of Joel 2, *(This is that!),* he spoke of his generation, but he also made the connection to our day. The prophet Joel had more to prophesy than the fulfillment of Peter's day. Joel also spoke of the latter rain. We now know that there was a great outpouring of the Holy Spirit in the first century, followed by a decline in power for a millennium to the depths of the "dark ages" Then with the Reformation God Himself began to restore "the years" verse 25.

The "V" of History

We can therefore view church history graphically as a huge "V" which began not with the apostles, but with Jesus, who was perfect everything. It ends with Jesus returning as the perfect bridegroom. However, the Church did not just keep getting better for 2,000 years. The graph started high and then plunged to the depths of evil before God began to restore, and will end at the highest point, the Second Coming. Between His appearances nothing was perfect. The first century believers were not perfect, but once removed. The deterioration had already begun. It was all down hill from then to the Dark Ages. Reformers began to receive revelation from God, of forgotten truth. This process continued into the 20th century, which I see as the mirror image of the first century in reverse order. Instead of getting worse, the true church has been getting better.

I see an outline of the 20th century in these three verses:

There are diversities of gifts, but the same Spirit. There are differences of ministries, but the same Lord. And there are diversities of activities, but it is the same God who works all in all (1 Cor. 12:4-6).

First was the restoration of the Holy Spirit and gifts in the early 1900's: *diversities of gifts, but the same Spirit.* This is the beginning of the latter rain that Joel had seen. Peter saw the early rain, but did not comment on the latter rain, because it was not relevant in his day.

In the 20th century, after the restoration of the Holy Spirit and gifts, the next stage was a very dry time spiritually. Two world wars, the great depression and the Holocaust broke up the fallow ground of humanity. In the middle of the century, following the Holocaust, a brief collective guilt of the nations opened the opportunity for God to birth Israel for the Jews, and reveal Jesus to the nations. Christians began to see Jesus not only as Savior, but as Lord: *differences of ministries, but the same Lord.* The year 1948 saw the restoration of the Lordship of Jesus through the revival of that day. If you went in to any tent revival then, you would have seen a banner over the platform: "Jesus Is Lord". This was also true in the 60's and 70's during the charismatic renewal. The most famous song of the charismatic renewal was the chorus: "He is Lord, He is Lord." This mid-century revival included the restoration of the gift ministries. It is amazing to note the evangelists who had their start around 1948 such as

Billy Graham, Oral Roberts, T.L. Osborne and others. The charismatic movement in the 1960's and 70's (around the time of Jerusalem's return to the Jews) saw the restoration of pastors and teachers. Even apostles and prophets have been recognized.

Then again, there was a spiritually dry period extending into the 90's, when this present revival was born with many special effects. YAHWEH is restoring the priesthood of believers at this time in history. God is restoring the revelation of Himself, His name YAHWEH, and His heart of the Father: *diversities of activities, but it is the same God who works all in all*. Consider a few examples: Toronto, Pensacola, Promise Keepers, Argentina, China, Russia and many other great outpourings. It is my opinion that we are in the last great revival of history, and that this will prove to be the most powerful, with the most saved of any single generation of history. This fascinating "V"-shaped view of history then culminates, not with us, who are still imperfect, but with the glorious return of Messiah Jesus, Who is the perfect Holy One!

The Israel Parallel

Parallel to all of this, God is restoring Israel. It started with the Balfour Declaration of 1917 during the Pentecostal birthing; then, Israel was born as a nation in 1948 in the Latter Rain movement; Jerusalem was restored to Israeli control in 1967 during the charismatic movement; and now the focus is on the Temple Mount. It is the book of Acts still happening! What great glories and what judgments await the earth! It is TIME. **We have reason for our faith** not only by the witness of the Holy Spirit and the Word, but also **by the relentless revelation of our God in history**. What a day to be alive! Moses, David, Ezekiel, Jeremiah, Isaiah, Elijah, Peter, John and Paul would love to be here in these days of fulfillment. This is what they were all waiting for, and we get to actually live through it! Think of it. The closing days of Bible history are now being written and we are here! Thank you Jesus and Abba, Father. Our faith is encouraged by such marvelous revelations in our day.

GOD IS FAITHFUL!

Chapter 4

Restoring the Name of YAHWEH

A recent sport's headline about Shaquille O'Neal, of NBA basketball fame declared: *My Name will be Remembered Forever.* Even though I highly doubt that Shaq's name will be remembered forever, it struck me as to how important a name is. Names like Elvis, Abe, FDR, Castro and Napoleon need no explanation. These names are chiseled into history and we are intimately familiar with the person and the events associated with the name. Yet, the most important name in the history of the universe is virtually unknown! The name of YAHWEH or Jehovah is used over 6,500 times in the original Hebrew text of the Old Testament. Why don't we see it there? What happened? Why don't we use His personal name?

The Unknown Name

The name of God has been forgotten. Some 300 years before Jesus began to teach, the name of God was sealed. By the time Jesus spoke the Sermon on the Mount, the name was known by few on that mount. It is fair to say that God's name was effectively banned from usage. Jesus told His disciples that persecutors would come because, "...*they do not know Him who sent Me*" John 15:21).

A Name Remembered

It is a name that lingers in the memory of God's people. Today, however, it is rarely used among His people in verse or in song. We are just now coming to the revelation of His name and are beginning to use His Name, YAHWEH. Given how much a person's name means to him, what do you think would happen if God personally appeared to you and you did not know His name; or worse yet, you called Him by another god's name? Names are important for identification, and Yahweh intends for His name to be known in the whole earth, even by the heathen. Sadly, there are few who acknowledge His name and fewer still who use it. What happened to cause men to forget the Name of God? Twenty-three centuries of tradition have obscured and even banned the use of the Name of God. These conditions exist whether in the synagogue or the church. Many proclaim through song and prose that we should magnify, praise and exalt the Name of God. But, in fact, they do not actually say His name! How ironic! Yes, there are some songs like: "Guide me O thou great Jehovah" but they are rare. New songs are starting to come out using Jehovah and even YAHWEH, but the general fact is still true that His personal name is missing.

Many in Christendom think the Name of God is Jesus. Jesus is the Son of God and yes, God the Son – But, *Jesus* is not the Name of God. The Name *Jesus* is a transliteration from the Latin which was translated from the Greek which was translated from the Hebrew. In the Hebrew language, His name is *Yeshua* which literally means "salvation". *And she will bring forth a Son, and you shall call His name JESUS, for He will save His people from their sins* (Matthew 1:21). Jesus is the Messiah, the Christ, the Savior! *Nor is there salvation in any other, for there is no other name under heaven given among men by which we must be saved* (Acts 4:12).

Father and Son

> *Who has ascended into heaven, or descended? Who has gathered the wind in His fists? Who has bound the waters in a garment? Who has established all the ends of the earth? What is His name, and what is His Son's name, If you know?* (Proverbs 30:4).

What is this about "His name" and "His Son's name"? How many Jews use the Father's name, YAHWEH? How many Christian's know that Jesus is the Son of God, but do not know or use the Father's name? We have no problem saying, "Jesus, Son of God." Yet it bothers us to say the same phrase in Hebrew: Yeshua ben YAHWEH. The word "God" is generic. It is used for any number of pagan, false gods. On the other hand, YAHWEH is absolutely definitive. There can be no mistaking that you are referring to the God of Abraham, Isaac, and Jacob; the God of Israel, the God of the whole Bible.

Fifty years ago in America, if anyone said "God" it was understood you were talking about the Bible God. Now however, you have to ask, "Which god?" They may be talking about the gods of Hinduism, Buddhism, Islam, or even humanism. Today, Islamic propaganda in the West takes advantage of our ignorance, by suggesting we all worship the same god, but their intent is to **seduce us** (see 1 John 2 below) into accepting the god of Islam. That god is not a father and does not have a son according to everything in their own sacred writings including the Koran itself. In fact, they are adamant about it. "Them's fightin' words, pardner!" as the movie cowboys used to say. These radical Muslims are killing for far less. To the confused Christians, YAHWEH declares: *You will have no other gods before Me!* " What part of this do we not get?

In most translations of the scriptures the Name of our God is cloaked. Rather than writing His name as Jehovah or YAHWEH it is written as "the LORD". This confusion and ambiguity about His Name did not take YAHWEH by surprise. Indeed, there is no doubt He was the One who cloaked His Name for a time. Now, in this last generation, it is clear in the prophetic scriptures that He desires to reveal His Name and His Son's name, Jesus. The Glory of YAHWEH will increase with the use of His Name and the name of His son. His deeds and His fame will be known throughout all the earth.

Define Antichrist

Continuing a bit further on the subject of the Father and Son, let's consider the Bible's own absolute definition of the antichrist. There may be many ideas of how to define that spirit of evil, but John the beloved apostle, inspired by the Holy Spirit, gave us the clearest revelation:

> *Who is a liar but he who denies that Jesus is the Christ? He is antichrist who denies the Father and the Son. Whoever denies the Son does not have the Father either; he who acknowledges the Son has the Father also. Therefore let that abide in you which you heard from the beginning. If what you heard from the beginning abides in you, you also will abide in the Son and in the Father. And this is the promise that He has promised us--eternal life. These things I have written to you concerning those who try to deceive you (KJV "seduce you")* (1 John 2:22-26).

It is always about the nature of God. My dear brother Sirus, a former Muslim who is now a pro-Israel Christian, recently made this true statement: "The Kingdom of God is relational, the world is transactional." The love relationship between the Father and Son, God and Jesus, YAHWEH and Yeshua, is the living example of life for us. To deny the Father OR the Son is the essence of antichrist. It has been said that the Muslim god demands you sacrifice your sons to die as martyrs' for him; but

YAHWEH gave His Son to die in your place, so that you may live! So choose life!

The Confusion

When suicide terrorists scream *Allah Akbar,* almost every mainline press report translates the Arabic phrase into "God is great." This is wrong on two counts. The phrase really should be translated "Allah is greater." The "God is great" translation plays into the common misconception that *Allah* is God and *Akbar* means great. This is a way of disassociating the terrorist from Islam and for the press to blame the whole terrorist thing on a generic god. It has another subtle effect of implying: "We all worship the same god." After all, isn't Allah just the Arabic word for God? No, it is the Arabic word for the *name* of the pagan god of Islam. Names mean something. In this case, it is life and death.

Many in the press lean to promoting this misconception because they do not believe in any god. It suits their bias and their agenda to lump all gods into one god. It promotes their goal of multiculturalism and their arrogant "neutrality" (an impossibility). They feel good that they have treated all religions the same. This makes them objective and, therefore, above the fray in their own opinion. They reject anyone who would contradict the conclusion that we all worship the same god. The press labels the people who know the living God as "hateful bigots," "narrow minded," "extreme right wingers" who lack "objectivity". The media draws a moral equivalence between Christians and terrorists. These subliminal suggestions come pouring out of the leftist press every night on the news.

How Far Do We Take This?

But, Allah is NOT the same as the God of Abraham, Isaac and Jacob and he is NOT the God of Jesus. The God of Abraham, Isaac and Jacob, has a name; it is YAHWEH (some pronounce His name Jehovah or Yehovah). Allah was a god selected from a plethora of desert gods that were common to the Arabian people dating back to the ancient Baal gods of the Canaanites. Mohammad came along in the seventh century peddling this moon god as the only god, and promoted his god, Allah, as the greatest: *Allah Akbar*. As I said above, it is not a benign phrase, but exalts and honors a specific pagan god who is completely **other** than YAHWEH. Furthermore, if you are still with me, we are told not to even *speak* the names of other gods!

And in all that I have said to you, be circumspect and make no mention of the name of other gods, nor let it be heard from your mouth (Exodus 23:13).

I have personally started my own little campaign to **not** use those other names except for teaching purposes. I submit to Exodus 23:13. Islam and its rise in the west is indeed one of the reasons that the personal name of God has become important. Not so long ago there was little doubt as to who God was. This was a Judeo-Christian nation and our God, whose name is YAHWEH, was seldom if ever confused with other demonic gods. This is no longer true. Yet, I am convinced that YAHWEH is allowing the rise of Islam not only for judgment for our moral and spiritual decay; but also for a redemptive purpose. He wants to show us and the whole world the glory of His great Name! Just as light shines brightest in the darkness, the name of YAHWEH will become famous in contrast with the character of the god of Islam and all the other gods.

Around 1995, after my first book "Prophesy to the Land!" was published, I received a letter from a Christian lawyer in Malaysia asking me about Allah being different from our God. He informed me that Bibles published by the Malaysian Bible Society actually used "Allah" as the translation of the Hebrew "YAHWEH". No wonder people are confused. The government of Malaysia is suing Christians for using Allah as the name of the Christian God. "Malaysia will lift a ban on the Malay edition of a Catholic newspaper if it agrees to stop using the word "Allah," an official said Thursday, but the editor of the paper rejected the precondition."[1]

In 2007, a Roman Catholic Bishop in the Netherlands, wanted people of all faiths to refer to God as "Allah."[2] Why not clear it up for everyone and just use the real names? That would be too easy.

YAHWEH IS THE FAITHFUL GOD!

[1] http://www.salon.com/wires/ap/world/2009/01/08/D95IRHB00 as malaysia catholic newspaper/index.html
[2] Roman Catholic Bishop Wants Everyone to Call God 'Allah' Thursday, August 16, 2007
http://www.foxnews.com/story/0,2933,293394,00.html

Chapter 5

The Cloaking

YAHWEH's name was not always cloaked. There was a time when YAHWEH was in common use among the people of God. God's name gradually slipped from common use after the time of Ezra and the rebuilding of the second temple. The name YAHWEH was first taken from the people around 350BC. The priests became the keeper of the name of YAHWEH and they uttered it only in prayer. By 291 BCE, the name of God had been removed from use. The high priest became the only one to speak His name and he did so only during Yom Kipper, when he went into the most Holy Place. Otherwise, he never so much as whispered the name, YAHWEH. It is interesting to note that even Rabbinic Judaism believes the Name will be pronounced once again when the Messiah reigns as King of the earth. May it be soon!

The final straw was the destruction of the second temple in 70 AD. No temple, no speaking of the name of YAHWEH. Despite the fact that YAHWEH is written 6,828 times in the Old Testament, no Orthodox rabbinic Jew has spoken the Name of Yahweh from then till now. Thus no one is sure of the Name's proper pronunciation. However, God wants us to use His name and is not that concerned about the "proper" pronunciation.

When I was first a Daddy and when Angel, my little baby girl, came toddling up to me and first said "Da-Da", I did not correct her saying, "No, No! It is Daddee!" I simply rejoiced and told everyone: "She said my name! She said my name!"

Somehow, I expect that is how God feels when we finally get personal with Him, whether it is YAHWEH, or Jehovah, or Yehovah, or Abba, or even Daddy. We have long invited people to come and know Jesus as their own personal Savior. I now invite you to come and know YAHWEH as your own personal intimate God and Father. When Jesus announced He was the Way, the Truth and the Life, He completed the declaration with *"No man comes to the Father, but through Me"* (John 14:6) Come to the Father, YAHWEH, and know Him personally! (For more on this subject, I highly recommend an excellent book: *A Prayer To Our Father* by Nehemia Gordon and Keith Johnson.)

Historical Perspective

In Rabbinic Judaism, there are three traditional reasons for not saying the name of God. (In fact, they do not use His name in print, either, even to the point of spelling God without the vowel: G-D.) The main reason is that they believe it is too holy to utter. The second is to avoid accidently taking His name in vain. Third, they are unsure how to pronounce it.

The Orthodox position is articulated quite clearly in an excellent article from *Rabbi Aryeh Kaplan's Handbook of Jewish Thought*, entitled: *Respecting God in Speech*. This particular article is a dissertation on how and why the name of God is not to be spoken. The following is an excerpt:

> *The Tetragrammaton is called God's "proper name" (Shem HaMeforash). Although God Himself is absolutely unknowable and unnamable, the Tetragrammaton is His highest emanation in creation. It is therefore considered most sacred, and is never pronounced as it is written, even in prayer. We are taught that one who pronounces the Tetragrammaton disrespectfully is worthy of death and has no portion in the World to Come. According to tradition, whenever the Tetragrammaton is written yud-hay-vov-hay, it is read Adonai. However, when it occurs in conjunction with the name Adonai, it is read Elohim."*

The article by Rabbi Kaplan goes on to say:

> *Originally, the Tetragrammaton was used by all the priests in their blessing. However, <u>there is a tradition that after Shimon HaTzaddik died in 3470 (291 BCE)</u>, its use was discontinued; since the Divine Presence (Shechina) was no longer*

manifest in the Temple and the other priests felt themselves unworthy.

This article can be found on Aish.com and a link is provided in the footnote below.[3]

YAHWEH in the New Testament

Since the name of God was hidden nearly 300 years before Jesus, what effect did that fact have on the Greek based writing of the New Testament? Written mostly in the First Century, were the apostles following the tradition of avoiding writing His name? I submit that they were. Throughout the Greek New Testament, the only word used for God is "kurios" which means "lord" or "master". This is true whether referring to Jesus or to the Father. Even direct quotes from the Old Testament, where God is clearly YAHWEH, the NT uses "lord". Therefore, I believe the Jewish tradition of obfuscating the name of YAHWEH, for whatever reason, was codified into the scriptures until it was all but lost. Today, few among Christians know that God even has a Name, and fewer still know what it is, or how it is pronounced. For a deeper analysis, I challenge you to do your own study of YAHWEH in the New Testament.

What Harm?

Great confusion as to who God is has infected the land. This tradition allowed His name to be eclipsed by other gods and by secular humanism. Even Presidents Bush and Obama publicly proclaimed that Muslims and

---

[3] http://www.aish.com/jl/kc/48931667.html

Christians worship the same God. This is completely false. This ignorance has caused tremendous harm. It is time for those who know His Name to proclaim YAHWEH as the Living God. God has an appointed time for everything under the sun. Now is the time for God's name to be glorified.

Quick Guide to Islam

After many years of study, The Lord gave me a very succinct summary of Islam contrasted with Christianity. I wrote a chapter, *The Baal gods and Islam*, on the subject in my first book. Here is what I consider to be the irreducible minimum:

We do *NOT* all worship the same God.

Islam's god is *not a father*, and has no son.

Islam's god is *not YAHWEH*, the God of Abraham, Isaac and Jacob.

> *Who has established all the ends of the earth? What is His name, and what is His Son's name, if you know?* (Proverbs 30:4).

The god of the Koran commands *your sons* to die for him.

The Living God of the Bible sent *His Son* to die for you.

> *For God so loved the world that He gave His only begotten Son, that whoever believes in Him should not perish but have everlasting life.* (John 3:16)

Choose life in Jesus!

And in all that I have said to you, be circumspect and make no mention of the name of other gods, nor let it be heard from your mouth. (Exodus 23:13)

Using the name of YAHWEH

It is high time we start practicing what we preach (and sing). I have been mystified for years how congregations can sing, *Clap your hands...*and not clap their hands! Or, *We bow before the Lord our Maker...* and not bow; Or *We raise our hands to You...* and not raise their hands. When I was growing up, we frequently sang a song named, "Standing on the Promises." A favorite saying of our worship leader was, "How can you sing 'Standing on the Promises' when you are sitting on the premises! Everyone, stand up!"

The same point can be made regarding using God's name. Just consider examples from the Psalms: *Sing to the name, lift your hands to the name, glorify the name,* or even *call upon the name.* Can you fulfill all these instructions without actually saying His name, YAHWEH?

*Because He has set his love upon me, therefore I will deliver him; I will set him on high, because he has **known My name.** He shall call upon Me, and I will answer him; I will be with him in trouble; I will deliver him and honor him. With long life I will satisfy him, And show him My salvation. (Psalm 91:14-16)*

GOD IS FAITHFUL!

Chapter 6

The Blessing of Knowing His Name

God first revealed his name to Moses. What a concept! God introduced Himself to Moses, who became the first man to know the name of God.

> *And God spoke to Moses and said to him: "I am YAHWEH. I appeared to Abraham, to Isaac, and to Jacob, as God Almighty, but by My name YAHWEH I was not known to them* (Exodus 6:2-3).

One of the most famous blessings in the Bible is the Aaronic Blessing (or the Aaronic Benediction). Look at it here with the actual name of God in place of the misleading translation "the LORD":

> *And YAHWEH spoke to Moses, saying: "Speak to Aaron and his sons, saying, 'This is the way you shall bless the children of Israel. Say to them: "YAHWEH bless you and keep you; YAHWEH make His face shine upon you, And be gracious to you; YAHWEH lift up His countenance upon*

you, And give you peace.' **"So they shall put My name on** *the children of Israel, and I will bless them"* (Number 6:22-27).

It ends with God's actual expressed intent to put His name on His people, so He could bless them! There is a direct connection between His name being used in functional application and His intent to bless Israel. To neglect using His name is almost as bad in effect, as to directly deny Him! Do you see it?

The Artist's Signature

We know the classic verse: *The earth is YAHWEH'S, and all its fullness, The world and those who dwell therein* (Psalm 24:1). But, did you know that when God finished His creation masterpiece, He signed it? I have a satellite photo on my wall that can be easily purchased in bookstores in Israel. It shows that from space you can actually see the name of YAHWEH (in Hebrew), formed by the dry riverbeds. This is at a place called Shiloh, in Samaria (also called the West Bank), near the modern towns of Nablus and Ramallah. The Hebrew letters of God's name are discernible in the land! Then consider this amazing text:

> *But go now to My place which was in Shiloh,* ***where I set My name at the first*** *(*Jeremiah 7:12a).

The Name of God is embossed on His creation. There is no other god who has created anything. The Creator God signed His creation at the place where Joshua first set up the Tabernacle in the Promised Land. What a God we serve! And we know His name. It is YAHWEH!

His Name is Famous

Only forty years after Moses is introduced to Yahweh, Rahab, a Canaanite harlot from Jericho, gained her place in God's hall of fame. This was precisely *because* she knew the name of YAHWEH. How, without television, internet, or radio did Rahab become so intimate with the name of God? Who is this heathen woman who feared God? She was not afraid to use the name of YAHWEH.

Now before they lay down, she came up to them on the roof, and said to the men: "I know that YAHWEH has given you the land, that the terror of you has fallen on us, and that all the inhabitants of the land are fainthearted because of you. For we have heard how YAHWEH dried up the water of the Red Sea for you when you came out of Egypt, and what you did to the two kings of the Amorites who were on the other side of the Jordan, Sihon and Og, whom you utterly destroyed. And as soon as we heard these things, our hearts melted; neither did there remain any more courage in anyone because of you, for YAHWEH your God, He is God in heaven above and on earth beneath. (Joshua 2:8-12)

There was no confusion in Rehab's mind as to who YAHWEH was. I wonder where she heard that Name? How did she know that it was YAHWEH that dried up the waters of the Red Sea? Folks must have been talking up the name of YAHWEH. God certainly didn't tell her but there was no doubt in Rahab's heathen mind that YAHWEH was God. The day will come again when the heathen will know and fear the name of YAHWEH.

Today, YAHWEH'S people have convinced themselves that they reverence the name of God by never using His name. Many of these same people, even some Christians, believe that Allah is the name of God or just another name for their God. They all nod in affirmation when the President says, "We all worship the same god." But God Himself will judge, because He has an opposing view to prevailing world opinion:

> How long will this be in the heart of the prophets who prophesy lies? Indeed they are prophets of the deceit of their own heart, who try to make My people forget My name by their dreams which everyone tells his neighbor, as **their fathers forgot My name for Baal** (Jeremiah 23:26-27).

This ancient sin of Israel is alive and well in our day! But Jehovah God has a better idea. He will again make His name famous!

Restoration of the Name of YAHWEH

The restoration of the name of YAHWEH is an awesome responsibility and I believe that through this restoration comes glory and power; manifested power, released to His people. This release is all in prophetic timing. This is the appointed time, the fullness of time for YAHWEH to make the difference between that which is holy and that which is not. Restoration is recognized in many areas of prophetic fulfillment. We see the gifts of the Holy Spirit, the Lordship of Jesus, and the Feasts of YAHWEH, all being restored before our eyes. The Land of Israel has been restored to the Jews. In the 1967 Six Day War, the gentiles lost their sovereignty over Jerusalem and no longer tread it down. Those who are not Jews have been reconciled to YAHWEH by accepting the Jewish Messiah as their own Savior. There are millions of former Muslims being saved through the blood of Jesus, the son of the father, YAHWEH. Now, even those who rejected Him (Israel) are accepting Him. Jews are coming in great numbers to recognize Yeshua (Jesus) as their Messiah and as Yeshua ben YAHWEH (Jesus, Son of God). This act brings life from the dead, resurrection power!

I say then, have they stumbled that they should fall? Certainly not! But through their fall, to provoke them to jealousy, salvation has come to the Gentiles. Now if their fall is riches for the world, and their failure riches for the Gentiles, how much more their fullness! For I speak to you Gentiles; inasmuch as I am an apostle to the Gentiles, I magnify my ministry, if by any means I may provoke to jealousy those who are my flesh and save some of them. For if their being cast away is the reconciling of the world, what

*will their acceptance be but life from the dead?
(Romans 11:11-15).*

This is RESURRECTION LIFE!

Hallelujah!

There is one instance where the name of God comes to the forefront in every language. This is in the use of the word *Hallelujah*. This word is transliterated from the Hebrew into every language. The word is the joining of two Hebrew words: *Hallel,* which means "praise", and *Yah,* which is short for YAHWEH. In the Bible, it is translated as "Praise the LORD!" Together Hallelujah means "praise YAHWEH. Even though His people, in ignorance, have stopped using His name, they actually still do use it every time they say Hallelujah. Isn't it just like God to hide His name in the mouth of His people?

Let me conclude this chapter with a true story that comes to me directly first person. My dear brother and friend, Jeff Ghiotto.[4] is an apostle sent out from Clearwater, Florida, to Latin America. He personally walks with the brother who experienced the following story.

A few years, ago a missionary to Brazil became burned out after many years of faithful service. He just became tired and went to the Lord and "resigned". He told Jesus he just could not go on any more. So, he drove several hours down a Brazilian road that came to a dead end at the edge of the Amazon jungle. There he spotted

---

[4] Check out Jeff's book, *Eye on the Horizon,* Columbus, Georgia, TEC Publications

a house for sale which he purchased for his "retirement". He moved into that house and had only lived there a few weeks before the remarkable encounter.

One day he saw an Amazon Indian step out of the jungle, which was adjacent to the back of his new property. He had considerable fear, not knowing the intentions of the Indian, who looked rather fearsome in his loincloth and primitive dress. He chose to greet the man, putting his trust in God for his safety. This native walked right up to him, and spoke in a dialect the missionary knew: "The Hallelujah God said you are supposed to tell us about Him!" Wow! The results, in the few years since that Chief came out of the jungle, is that over 3,000 Amazon Indians came to salvation in Jesus! HALLELUJAH! It is amazing what YAHWEH can do during our "retirement." May His name become famous again!

GOD IS FAITHFUL!

Chapter 7

SPEAK TO THE DIRT

The next three chapters are a close look at Ezekiel 36, which Christians view as a spiritual analogy of salvation. But taken literally, it declares the promises of God to the physical land and people of Israel. My early mentor, Earl Waterman, always said: "If you can possibly take a scripture passage literally, do so." This is especially true of Ezekiel 36.

Before we can discuss the people of promise, we must start with the covenant land. God called Ezekiel to prophesy the Word of the Lord. This account in the book of Ezekiel seems a bit odd at first glance, when taken literally. God sent Ezekiel around the land talking to inanimate objects. It is bad enough when you talk to yourself, but here is a man speaking to dirt. It was not easy being a prophet of God. Ezekiel was commissioned to deliver his message to mountains, rivers, valleys, cliffs, trees, rocks and even cities. This has to be one of the more bewildering assignments ever given to a prophet of God.

Ezekiel 36:1 confirms my point:
> And you son of man, prophesy to the mountains of Israel and say, "O mountains of Israel, hear the word of YAHWEH!" In verse 4 it continues: therefore, O mountains of Israel, hear the word of the Lord YAHWEH! Thus says the Lord YAHWEH to the mountains, the hills, the rivers, the valleys, the desolate wastes, and the cities that have been forsaken, which became plunder and mockery to the rest of the nations all around. And finally in verse 6: Therefore prophesy concerning the **land** of Israel, and say to the mountains, the hills, the rivers, and the valleys.

We are interested in exactly what the prophecy says, but first, just pause and absorb the fact, that the prophecy is directed not to people, but to the "dirt!" It is necessary to emphasize this point so we can understand that the promise is not simply to an ethnic people, but to an actual geographical location on the globe.

There are three reasons why this fact is significant. First, the geographical orientation of the promise indicates that we should not lean to a symbolic or spiritualized interpretation of the prophecy. Second, the geography is evidence that God's promises to the people of Israel do not stand alone, but are directly connected to previously established promises to the land. The third and most important reason is what this promise says about the character of God. He is the God who *keeps* His word. Earlier, Ezekiel clearly makes the same point:

> "*For* **on** *My holy mountain,* **on** *the mountain height of Israel," says the Lord YAHWEH, "***there** *all the house of Israel, all of them in the land, shall serve Me;* **there** *I will accept them,"* (Ezek.20:40).

The words emphasized are geographical words. They refer to the land. God has made certain promises to the land that must be kept, not for the peoples' sake, but for the integrity of the One who said it.

Isaiah 62:4 uses even stronger language:

> *You shall no longer be termed Forsaken, Nor shall your* **land** *any more be termed Desolate; But you shall be called Hephzibah,* **and your land Beulah;** *For YAHWEH delights in you,* **And your land shall be married.**

Beulah is the Hebrew word for *married.* God is revealing that His commitment to the land is a marriage covenant. He does not lightly use such an analogy. God is married to the *land* of Israel as a specific geographic entity in the earth.

THE NATURE OF GOD

God's covenant nature is revealed in the following verse.

Therefore know that YAHWEH your God, He is God, the faithful God who keeps covenant and mercy for a thousand generations with those who love Him and keep His commandments; (Deut. 7:9).

This is a monumental declaration of the nature of God. It is what theologians call an immutable fact. It cannot be canceled, debated, or contradicted. God faithfully *keeps* His word. Some believe that the second half of the verse is a loophole allowing God to break His word, if the people of some future generation stop loving Him and break His commandments. This is where you must think very carefully. You dare not misunderstand this point. An individual person or even a group may be lost through unbelief, but the original promise to Abraham and the fathers *must be kept,* regardless of individuals who choose to reject God's grace. YAHWEH will continue to have mercy on the descendants of Abraham, Isaac and Jacob because He said He would. Of course, the promise considered in this chapter concerns the *land* of Israel. The promise to the people comes later.

THE OATH OF GOD

There is another aspect of this subject which must be seen before we go on to specifics about the people. No less than three references are made in Ezekiel and Isaiah, to God raising His hand in an oath. Let us consider each one in context.

I have set watchmen on your walls, O Jerusalem, Who shall never hold their peace day or night. You who make mention of YAHWEH, do not keep silent, And give Him no rest till He establishes And till He makes Jerusalem a praise in the earth. YAHWEH has sworn by His right hand And by the arm of His strength: "Surely I will no longer give your grain To be food for your enemies; And the sons of the foreigner shall not drink your new wine, For which you have labored. But those who have gathered it shall eat it, And praise YAHWEH; Those who have brought it together shall drink it in My holy courts." (Isaiah 62:6-9).

This promise includes the people, but is directed to the *physical land*, and the *produce of the land,* as well as the *specific city* of Jerusalem.

There is a second reference to God lifting His hand in an oath.

*Then you shall know that I am YAHWEH, when I bring you into the **land** of Israel, into the **country** for which I lifted My hand in an oath to give to your fathers* (Ezekiel 20:42).

We will cover Ezekiel 20 in more detail later when we consider the peculiar phenomena that all the Jews who are leaving the nations to which they have been scattered, do not automatically return directly to Israel. Nevertheless, we see another reference to God raising His Hand in an oath. Again there is a mention of the land, but this time He adds the word *country* so there can be no mistake His promise is geographical.

The third example of this remarkable phrase is found in the chapter which joins the land and the people.

> *Therefore thus says the Lord YAHWEH: "I have lifted My hand in an oath that surely the nations that are around you shall bear their own shame. But you, O mountains of Israel, you shall shoot forth your branches, and yield your fruit to My people Israel, for they are about to come."* (Ezekiel 36:7-8).

The first seven verses of Ezekiel 36 are not about the people at all, but about the land. God is speaking to the physical land, the literal geographical place. When YAHWEH uses the personal pronoun *you* in verse 7, He is still referring to the land. Even in verse 8, where He first refers to the people, the subject is still the land. His oath is clearly to the land.

God swearing by an oath and by His uplifted hand, has to be one of the most profound concepts in the Bible. Just picture it. The Holy Almighty God deems that this promise is so important that He swears to it! The idea of God swearing an oath was such a curiosity to me that I consulted *Strong's Concordance* and was amazed to discover no less than 55 Bible verses which refer to God swearing to keep His word to the land and people of Israel. No other oath was systematically recorded even close to 55 times. Note this New Testament passage:

> *For when God made a promise to Abraham, because He could swear by no one greater, He swore by Himself, saying, "Surely blessing I will*

*bless you, and multiplying I will multiply you."
And so after he had patiently endured, he
obtained the promise. For men indeed swear by
the greater, and an oath for confirmation is for
them an end of all dispute. Thus God,
determining to show more abundantly to the
heirs of promise the immutability of His counsel,
confirmed it by an oath, that by two immutable
things, in which it is impossible for God to lie, we
might have strong consolation who have fled for
refuge to lay hold of the hope set before us"*
(Hebrews 6:13-18).

The two unchangeable (immutable) things are the
original promise itself (based on God's character), and
then the oath sworn by God to confirm His promise
(based on His spoken Word). These are both resting on
the unchangeable fact that it is *impossible* for God to lie.

THE IMMUTABILITY OF GOD

I would like to define the word *immutable* for you in
such a way that you will never forget. In fact, you will
remember it from now on, every time you pick up your
television remote control. The definition of *immutable* was
a difficult concept for me to understand. The light came
on for me when I thought of it in modern usage. Let's
face it: nobody uses the word *immutable* in daily
conversation. Then I remembered my TV remote control.
What is your favorite button on your remote control?
Whenever I preach this message, I ask the congregation
to respond. Some simply like the "on/off" button. Others

like the channel changers; but most people agree with me. My favorite remote control button is the "mute" button. It is so convenient. It seems to give me a sort of power - yes, even *control* over the television! If I don't like listening to a commercial, I just push the "mute" button and I don't have to listen. Don't you agree? Even if you prefer the "on/off" button or the channel changer button, you can see my point. There is a definite sense of control over what you see and hear.

The problem is that many live their lives as though God generated a great cosmic broadcast that they could tune in/tune out, turn on/turn off; change, or mute on a whim with their trusty little remote control devices. Many people don't like what God says or does. They don't want to hear His voice, so they try everything to mute Him; but sooner or later God makes Himself heard. *You can't mute God - He is immutable!* They try to make Him fit into their box. They try to change the message to something more to their liking, but it is impossible. He is unchangeable. He is in control. James 1:17 says of Him: *...with whom there is no variation or shadow of turning.* Malachi 3:6 quotes the Lord: *For I am YAHWEH, I do not change...* and that great declaration in Hebrews 13.8 that says: *Jesus Christ is the same yesterday, today, and forever.* **God is immutable!**

The apostle Paul spoke this principle in another context.

> *Therefore, when I was planning this, did I do it lightly? Or the things I plan, do I plan according*

to the flesh, that with me there should be Yes, Yes, and No, No? But as God is faithful, our word to you was not Yes and No. For the Son of God, Jesus Christ, who was preached among you by us - by me, Silvanus, and Timothy - was not Yes and No, but in Him was Yes. For all the promises of God in Him are Yes, and in Him Amen, to the glory of God through us. (I Cor.1:17-20).

Not only does Paul confirm the principle of God's truthfulness and faithfulness, but he also declares that *all* of God's promises are still *yes* in Jesus!

God has promised to restore the land of Israel. This is not a conditional or temporary promise. No, He will continue to bring it to pass even to a thousand generations and will fulfill it through Jesus to the end of time. The trustworthiness of its fulfillment does not depend on any people--past, present or future--but on the *character* of the immutable God with whom it is impossible to lie. So if our God of truth, YAHWEH, raises His hand to signify the earnestness of His heart-given promise, we know He means it and will do exactly as He says. *We cannot mute God!*

GOD IS FAITHFUL!

Chapter 8

The Everlasting Covenant

Theologians make a serious mistake when they conclude that Israel has been *permanently* rejected on the basis of her sin. She is properly judged for her sin, which is characterized by God in Ezekiel 36 as profane and adulterous. In fact, the judgment eventually lasts nearly 2,000 years. But the error is to say that this chastisement is *permanent.* This mistake is like a space probe that is sent off at an error of only one degree, but that misses its mark by millions of miles at the other end of its mission. The angle of error is a constant, but the distance from the desired course grows wider the farther away the probe travels from the genesis point. We are talking about a very critical and fundamental aspect of God's plan. Does His purpose turn on the whims and vagaries of man? Does He discard plans and blueprints like some cosmic mad scientist? Certainly the scriptures reveal individual judgment, but God is able to judge between the unrepentant and the repentant within the same family. Let's start with the *people* of promise in

Ezekiel 36. God will have mercy and restore their place in the end, because He is committed to keeping His word to their Fathers.

The Issue

The issue, therefore, is not the state of individual Jews, or even generations of rebellion, but the covenant oath of YAHWEH, the immutable, unchangeable God. There is no doubt that the Jewish people have certainly sinned against God, but of course, this is true for all of us. Is it not? *For all have sinned and fall short of the glory of God* (Romans 3:23). And, *As it is written: "There is none righteous, no, not one."* (Romans 3:10). This was quoted by Paul directly from the Old Testament:

> *The fool has said in his heart, "There is no God." They are corrupt, and have done abominable iniquity; There is none who does good. God looks down from heaven upon the children of men, To see if there are any who understand, who seek God. Every one of them has turned aside; They have together become corrupt; There is none who does good, No, not one"* (Psalm 53:1-3).

The issue is not who will behave or who won't behave, but "What has God said?" The ultimate outcome is based on the character and ability of the One who promised. The error of one degree is to focus on the object of His love, instead of the *source* of that love in His loving nature. That mistake causes us to miss the point by a millions of miles. Therefore, I have faith for the land

and people of Israel, *not* because of their behavior, but because of the oath of YAHWEH. The entire infrastructure of Scripture depends absolutely upon the veracity of YAHWEH, the One who spoke it. If God's oath in Ezekiel 36 was a lie, or has been broken, or ever will be revoked, then we have no basis for believing anything He says! If the One who gave the oath broke it, then our hope for salvation through Jesus is vain. If God is a covenant breaker -- even if just one time -- then His absolute nature of faithfulness is compromised, and His word cannot logically be trusted on any point. I know this is a hard word, but it is critical to our faith.

Do you see my point? The truthful God cannot lie!

God is not a man, that He should lie, Nor a son of man, that He should repent. Has He said, and will He not do it? Or has He spoken, and will He not make it good? (Numbers 23:19)

*God faithfully keeps covenant and mercy for a **thousand generations*** (Deut. 7:9).

Again in Psalm 105:8-10 the scripture says,

*He remembers His covenant forever, The word which He commanded, for a **thousand generations**, The covenant which He made with Abraham, And His oath to Isaac, And confirmed it to Jacob for a statute, To Israel for an **everlasting covenant.***

Another important principle is expressed in this passage:

For I am YAHWEH. I speak, and the word which
I speak will come to pass; it will no more be
postponed; for in your days, O rebellious house,
I will say the word and perform it (Ezek. 12:25).

This means that God not only speaks the word, but He is also the One who makes it happen! At some point in history (which someone has succinctly defined as "His-story"), God will bring about the precise fulfillment of His promise. It is God who speaks a word and it is God who will bring it to pass. The exact manner and *timing* of His word being fulfilled may well be debatable. But the *fact* of it is as sure as the God who said it. We may not like it, but we had better not try to tinker with the pre-ordained intentions of the Creator. If we do, we will find ourselves as off course as that space probe mentioned earlier.

The divine nature of God is unchangeable. The prophet Malachi links that fact to the continued existence of the descendants of Jacob: *For I am YAHWEH, I do not change; **Therefore** you are not consumed, O sons of Jacob* (Mal. 3:6). He is teaching them that if it were up to their behavior, God would have wiped them out! The only reason He has not consumed them, is because He gave His word to their fathers and He does not change. This divine characteristic is also seen in reference to Jesus: *Jesus Christ is the same yesterday; today, and forever.* (Heb. 13:8). It is reinforced again in the Book of James.

Every good gift and every perfect gift is from
above, and comes down from the Father of

lights, with whom there is no variation or shadow of turning (James 1:17).

There is *no variation or shadow of turning* with God! He will never deviate one degree from the precise foreordained destiny of His purpose not only for Israel, but for all creation.

A Rebellious Nation

Ezekiel the prophet was called to his ministry with a mandate to speak the YAHWEH'S message whether or not the people received it:

> *Then the Spirit entered me when He spoke to me, and set me on my feet; and I heard Him who spoke to me. And He said to me: "Son of man, I am sending you to the children of Israel, to a rebellious nation that has rebelled against Me; they and their fathers have transgressed against me to this very day. For they are impudent and stubborn children, I am sending you to them, and you shall say to them 'Thus says the Lord YAHWEH.' As for them, whether they hear or whether they refuse - for they are a rebellious house - yet they will know that a prophet has been among them"* (Ezek. 2:2-5).

They will know that a *prophet* has been among them! God delights in revealing His plans. His people -- then or now -- may not heed His warnings, but God will always raise up prophets to declare His truth.

Multiplication

Now, we return to Ezekiel 36, which we left in the middle of the prophet's message to the land. This land message does not end in verse 8, but continues on through verse 15 - at which point God's prophecy is extended to include the *people* of the land. Although He still speaks to the land in verses 8-15, several references are made about the people:

> *they are about to come* (v.8); *I will multiply men upon you* (v.10); *I will multiply upon you man and beast; and they shall increase and bear young; I will make you inhabited as in former times, and do better for you than at your beginnings* (v.11); *Yes, I will cause men to walk on you, My people Israel; they shall take possession of you, and you shall be their inheritance; no more shall you bereave them of their children* (v.12).

Remember that the personal pronoun "you" in each of these verses refers to the land. God links the restoration of the people of Israel to keeping His covenant with the land of Israel. This prophecy has never been fulfilled and thus remains for these last days. We know it is talking about the final regathering because of the finality in key words used throughout the chapter such as "no more" "anymore," "scattered," and "dispersed." Also, over and over he uses the plural, "nations" and "countries," as well as "*all* countries," which is a very significant clue. This cannot refer to the other historical captivities where Israel was taken each time to a specific single nation, as in the cases of Egypt and Babylon. The only restoration of Israel that fits the language of Ezekiel 36 is the great scattering or Diaspora of the two millennia since Jesus' earthly ministry. The outcasts of Israel have in historical fact been scattered to all the nations only in this final dispersion. The previous judgments each featured capture and exile to a single country. However, beginning with the era of the Roman Empire and in every generation since then till the present, they have been literally scattered among all the nations.

It is miraculous that their Jewish identity was maintained for two thousand years. No matter how hard they tried to assimilate, they were still Jews. A contemporary paradox illustrates this point. In Israel, the rules spelling out who is a Jew can get rather technical and it often becomes a debatable issue. Some of the Russian Jews who escaped to Israel in the 90's found it difficult to prove their Jewish identity. Yet in Russia there was no such debate. Every Russian Jew has a "J" stamped on his identity papers, which leads to serious problems of anti-Semitic discrimination and persecution. How ironic that Jews suffering so much at the hands of the Russian officials are then challenged as to their "Jewishness" when they arrive in the Promised Land! (There are, of course, some legitimate security concerns for Israel in avoiding infiltration. There are also financial reasons for the Israelis to be careful about admitting new immigrants, since every returning Jew is given substantial monetary subsidy under the Law of Return.)

Beginning in verse 16 of Ezekiel 36, The God of Israel gives another prophecy to the man of God, this time for the *people*. These verses will be explained more in the next chapter. However, there are a few more verses to examine in the light of YAHWEH multiplying men. First in verse 24:

> *For I will take you from among the nations, gather you out of all countries, and bring you into your own land.*

Verse 28 says,

> *Then you shall dwell in the land that I gave to your fathers; you shall be My people, and I will be your God.*

The chapter ends with this beautiful and profound promise in verses 37-38:

> *Thus says the Lord YAHWEH: "I will also let the house of Israel inquire of Me to do this for them: I will increase their men like a flock. Like a flock offered as holy sacrifices, like the flock at Jerusalem on its feast days, so shall the ruined cities be filled with flocks of men. Then they shall know that I am YAHWEH."*

I have witnessed this phenomena myself. Each time I return to visit Israel, there are more people. The increase in Israeli population of a million and a half people, since 1990, would be like the United States receiving over 75 million new immigrants in the same period. In 1990 I had the privilege of speaking to a Messianic congregation in

Tiberias that had just grown from 260 to 300 (mostly Israeli) believers by the addition of forty Russian Pentecostal Jews who had recently obtained their citizenship. What joy we shared as their Siberian pastor, who could speak no English, hugged and kissed my neck, an American pastor who could speak no Russian. It was truly a foretaste of Divine glory.

GOD IS FAITHFUL!

Chapter 9

No Plan B

Was God surprised and taken off guard when Adam and Eve fell into sin? Did that event throw a monkey wrench into God's "little earth experiment"? Did He wring his hands and worry: "What am I going to do? Oh! What am I going to do now? I wasn't prepared for this." Does God have a Plan A and B and perhaps a Plan C or D? Of course it sounds foolish when put this way, but has God ever been surprised by any development of history? This is a very critical and basic issue. This question is also pertinent to our whole story. If God just tries a plan "to see if it works" and in fact does not really know whether it will, then He is not the God of the Bible.

> Remember the former things of old, For I am God, and there is no other; I am God, and there is none like Me, Declaring the end from the beginning, And from ancient times things that are not yet done, saying, "My counsel shall stand, And I will do all My pleasure," Calling a

bird of prey from the east, The man who executes My counsel from a far country. Indeed I have spoken it; I will also bring it to pass, I have purposed it; I will also do it (Isaiah 46:9-11).

This hardly sounds like a God who is ruling at the whims of mankind's vacillating will. We do have a free will as it affects our personal place in God's plan, but our choices will neither alter nor thwart God's purpose. He is the only One who knows the outcome from beginning to end before it happens!

Declaring the end from the beginning, And from ancient times things that are not yet done, Saying, 'My counsel shall stand, And I will do all My pleasure, " (Isaiah 46:10).

There is no Plan B!

Some Christians today are being tempted with the so-called "replacement theology" which concludes that it didn't work out with Israel, so God raised up the Church to replace them. The danger of this line of thinking is that if God could change His mind about His promises to Israel, what would keep Him from changing His mind about the Church? Most people in the Western nations are ignorant of Islam, but Islamic theology teaches precisely that! They say Israel blew it and then God called the Church, but they blew it too, so God called Mohammed and the Muslims of Islam. In effect, they teach that Islam is Plan C. This is not true! ***God does not change His plan to fit man, but He changes***

man to fit His plan. He has had only one plan from the beginning, and ultimately He will fulfill it, either with us or without us. In the end there will be an Israel in the ancient land fulfilling in exact literal detail every promise of the Bible. These promises work in concert, not in conflict, with the promises to the Church in all nations.

The Old and New Covenants are a progressive revelation of the original blueprint. These testaments are not mutually exclusive or contradictory as some teach, but are a beautifully woven tapestry. They reveal the infinite artistry of our loving Creator Who is revealed most perfectly in Jesus, the Alpha and the Omega, the beginning and the end. Jesus is not only the Omega of the New Testament, but He is also the Alpha of the Old Testament. God has been working on only one plan all along and it is right on schedule. Israel has always been in the plan and still is, even at the end. We, the Church, can only understand how we fit in the plan by understanding the context of Israel. The Church is grafted into Israel, the original planting of the Lord. There is no new tree! There is no Plan B!

Jesus was a Jew. The first apostles were Jewish. The early Church was Jewish. The drift away from our Jewish roots in Israel can be attributed partially to the success of evangelism. By sheer numbers, the believers are now overwhelmingly formerly Gentile by birth and culture. But this does not cancel our Jewish roots. The Jerusalem Council in Acts 15 had great bearing on our contemporary situation. If new believers (formerly Gentiles) were not required to be Judaized, then new Jewish believers today need not be "Gentilized". We require far too much cultural conformity to non-biblical church traditions. Can a Jew remain culturally Jewish and still believe in Jesus? Does he have to "buy in" to all of our traditions? Is there a proper role for Messianic Judaism in contemporary Christianity? (For an excellent, comprehensive treatment of the subject of Messianic Judaism I recommend *The Messianic Church Arising!* by Dr. Robert D. Heidler.) [5]

Conditional vs. Unconditional

There are different types of promises. Sometimes God says *if you* do this or that, then *He will* do such and such. This promise is conditional. There are unconditional promises where God swears with no conditions, no "if". God's promises dealt with in this book are unconditional, have never been nullified, and will be precisely fulfilled. This fulfillment does not ignore Israel's sinful behavior; but on the contrary, includes the acknowledgment of her profane and "unacceptable" record. God does not imply that Israel is not judged. He clearly *links* their scattering or Diaspora as the proper judgment.

> *Therefore I poured out My fury on them for the blood they had shed on the land, and for their idols with which they had defiled it. So I scattered them among the nations, and they were dispersed throughout the countries; I*

---

[5] Dr. Robert D. Heidler, *The Messianic Church Arising!* Denton, Texas, Glory of Zion International Ministries.

judged them according to their ways and their deeds (Ezekiel 36:18-19).

He scattered them and judged them righteously because they deserved it.

Even in the dispersion, Israel continued to sin. This point is given five-fold emphasis in Ezekiel 36:20-23. The first occurs in verse 20:

*wherever they went, they **profaned** My holy name.*

The second follows in verse 21:

*But I had concern for My holy name, which the house of Israel had **profaned** among the nations wherever they went.*

And again, it says in verse 22,

*My holy name's sake, which you have **profaned**,*

and finally it is mentioned twice (the fourth and fifth occurrences) in verse 23:

*And I will sanctify My great name which has been **profaned** among the nations, which you have **profaned** in their midst.*

The premise that Israel's sin could utterly remove her contradicts this unconditional promise. If the promise depended upon Israel's behavior, she certainly would have been permanently rejected. But again and again, in this passage, and throughout the Bible, God expresses his mercy and grace based on His character alone. He keeps

His word. He is always faithful even when Israel or the Church is not.

Bypassed or Restored?

Another profound linkage is revealed in this passage. God first links their sin to their dispersion, but then He plainly links their regathering *not* to their behavior, but to His Holy Name, YAHWEH! He must uphold the integrity of the promises He gave to their fathers.

> *I do not do this for your sake, O house of Israel, but for My holy **name's** sake...* (Ezekiel 36:22).

Again in verse 32 it says:

> *Not for your sake do I do this, says the Lord YAHWEH, let it be known to you. Be ashamed and confounded for your own ways, O house of Israel!*

But God's great plan will be fulfilled, not in *bypassing* them, but by *saving* them. That is the miracle that reveals the glory of God.

> *And I will sanctify My great **name,** which has been profaned among the nations, which you have profaned in their midst; and the nations shall know that I am YAHWEH, says the Lord YAHWEH, **when** I am hallowed in you before their eyes* (Ezekiel 26:23).

The *nations* will know God is YAHWEH *when* He is considered holy or hallowed by Israel in front of the eyes of the nations. This truly is the amazing grace of the faithful God. The apostle Paul saw this promise also:

> *For if their being cast away is the reconciling of the world, what will their acceptance be but life from the dead?* (Romans 11:15).

There is no Plan B.

Ezekiel 36 lists many unconditional promises and some are very specific. As we continue reading in verse 24, the Lord indicates that the regathering of the people of Israel to the land of Israel will be followed by a supernatural work of God in them. God will do seven supernatural works to restore them to relationship with Him in verses 25-26:

1. He will "sprinkle clean water" on them (which I take to indicate the outpouring of the Holy Spirit on them).

2. He will "cleanse" them from "filthiness."

3. He will "cleanse" them from "all idols."

4. He will "give" them a "new heart."

5. He will "put a new spirit within" them.

6. He will remove their "heart of stone."

7. He will give them a "heart of flesh."

I will put My Spirit within you and cause you to walk in My statutes, and you will keep My judgments and do them. Then you shall dwell in the land that I gave to your fathers; you shall be

My people, and I will be your God. I will deliver
you from all your uncleannesses.   (Ezekiel
36:27-29).

This supernatural personal restoration leads to their permission to dwell in the land in this restored relationship with God, complete with seven more specific *blessings* in verses 29-31.

1. Multiplied grain.

2. No famine.

3. Multiplied fruit.

4. Increased harvest in their fields.

5. Never again bear the reproach of nations due to famine.

6. Remembrance of evil ways. (I see this as a blessing because those who forget the mistakes of history are destined to repeat those mistakes.)

7. Self-loathing. (This is the recognition of the nature of unredeemed man and is a necessary prerequisite leading to repentance and salvation.)

One More List

Finally, lest we be tempted in any way to spiritualize this passage and these promises, YAHWEH brings us back to the land in verse 33. The theme at the start of Ezekiel 36 was the land, and the prophecy ends with *seven blessings on the land!*

1. The cities and ruins will be rebuilt.

2. The land will be tilled.

3. The desolate land will be like the Garden of Eden.

4. The cities will be fortified.

5. The cities will be inhabited.

6. The nations will know that it was YAHWEH Who did the rebuilding.

7. The cities will be filled with flocks of men.

God tells the prophet Ezekiel in verse 36 to prophesy for Him in the first person: *I, YAHWEH, have spoken it, and I will do it.* Then finally in verse 38 he speaks for God again: *Then they shall know that I am YAHWEH.* There is an unmistakable aspect of this story that, by necessity, includes the prophetic voice of God. I believe that there is destined to be a great revival harvest of lost souls at the end of the age. Much of it will result from the people of God today lifting up their voices to prophesy the Word of the Lord. There are certainly very specific restraints and protections given in Scripture about how to judge contemporary prophesies. The rules are not given to eliminate prophetic declarations, but rather, to set them apart. If God's intention was to eliminate the gifts, there would have been no point to include such specific rules in the Bible such as 1 Corinthians 12-14. God is still speaking through His prophetic voice today by the power and manifestation of His Holy Spirit. We should rejoice for the current revival. However, not all are happy about what God is doing with Israel...

GOD IS FAITHFUL!

Chapter 10

God Is Faithful

A new wave of anti-Israel theology is gaining credibility in the United States. This ideology has raised controversial questions about Israel, shaking the theology of many American Christians. This teaching goes so far as to deny the scope or even the historical fact of the Holocaust. Under the banner of "replacement theology," these doctrines reiterate heresies that many of us hoped had died in that World War II bunker with Adolph Hitler and his "solution to the Jewish problem."

In a book titled *To Whom Is God Betrothed?*[6] the author purported to discuss "the Biblical basis for the church's support of national Israel." He instead proceeded to detail why he believed the Church should *not* support the nation of Israel today. He used Scripture to defend his case, but he misused the Scriptures to give homage to

---

[6] Earl Paulk, *To Whom Is God Betrothed* (Atlanta, Georgia: Dimension Publishers, 1985)

tired old arguments that would be better left in the Dark Ages.

Three particular questions deserve to be examined:

- Do the Jews *alone* bear the guilt for killing Jesus Christ?

- Did God thereafter divorce His Jewish bride and marry the Church as a second wife?

- Is God through with Israel as a chosen, unique covenant people?

The heresy suggested by these three questions may not be immediately apparent, so allow me to explain. The first question of Israel's singular guilt potentially undermines the basic doctrine that "all have sinned." An affirmative answer to the second question would make God a polygamist or divorced with a new bride. The third issue undermines the nature of God as the One who *keeps* His covenants. These three questions challenge biblical orthodoxy and are each worthy of further scrutiny.

Are the Jews Alone Responsible?

Let us examine the first question. Are the Jews *alone* responsible for Jesus' death? No, one of the most heinous charges throughout history has been the self-righteous and arrogant epithet "Christ-Killers!" which was hurled at Jews during the Crusades, the Spanish Inquisition, and Hitler's Holocaust. Even today in the inner cities of any metropolitan area around the world where Israel has been scattered, young Gentiles still mock and spit upon young Hebrew boys for the same reason. Jews are one of many ethnic groups that suffer prejudice, but they are unique in the religious basis of the abuse. They are victims of a generalized condemnation of an entire people group as being responsible for killing the world's Savior. No single person can defend himself from such an absolute judgment.

Yet, the question remains, and deserves an honest answer: Are the Jews *alone* the ones who killed Jesus? Let the Scriptures enlighten us. Consider that the company of believers quoted from Exodus 2 and Psalm 2 in their prayer upon the release of Peter and John.

> *So when they heard that, they raised their voice to God with one accord and said: "YAHWEH, You are God, who made heaven and earth and the sea, and all that is in them, who by the mouth of Your servant David have said: 'Why did the nations rage, And the people plot vain things? The kings of the earth took their stand, And the rulers were gathered together Against YAHWEH and against His Christ.'*
>
> *For truly against Your holy Servant Jesus, whom You anointed, **both** Herod and Pontius Pilate, **with the Gentiles** and the people of Israel, were gathered together **to do whatever Your hand and Your purpose determined before to be done*** (Acts 4:24-28).

There are two undeniable facts revealed in this passage. First, *both Jew and Gentile* killed Christ. Second, it was the purpose of God! Clearly, the answer to question one is "No." Paul warns Gentiles in Romans 11:18 when speaking of the Jewish branch temporarily broken off: *do not boast against the branches...* In verses 20 and 21 he warns further:

> *...Do not be haughty, but fear. For if God did not spare the natural branches, He may not spare you either.*

Some Christians would judge and punish the Jews, but nowhere in the Bible are we given that assignment. The sovereign God has reserved that right to Himself; He is the only One to vindicate His plan. He knows that we are all guilty before Him and His final word is this: *...Vengeance is mine, I will repay! says the Lord* (Rom. 12:19). Our plea should be for mercy -- for ourselves and for the Jewish people.

Did God Divorce Israel?

This second question concerns the Bride of Christ. The "new wave" theology in question does not dispute that Israel was God's wife in the Old Testament. They contend that God has broken His marriage covenant with His Jewish bride because of her unfaithfulness and sin. The notion says that God, having put away His first wife, Israel, is now betrothed to a new bride, the Church.

Yet Jesus says that Moses only permitted divorce because of the hardness of your heart (Mark 10:5). God's heart is not hardened! Hosea reveals the classic illustration of God's heart toward Israel. The anti-Israel view has God divorcing Israel as Hosea divorced his adulterous wife. This view teaches that God permanently broke His covenant with Israel, but He did not. Hosea did divorce Gomer, but the end of the story is overlooked. In the end, both Gomer and Israel are restored (see Hosea 2:14 to 3:5 and chapter 14). In every generation there have been literal descendants of Israel who have embraced faith in God. God has always had a remnant no matter how small, and has thereby continually maintained His covenant. God is faithful even when we are not! He is able to save to the uttermost all those who call on Him! He is the Redeemer, the One who keeps His promises. Don't make Him like one of us. YAHWEH is not made in man's image.

Paul quotes Isaiah 59:20, saying God will yet keep His covenant with Israel to "*turn away ungodliness from Jacob*". The name *Jacob* is used, so it is absolutely clear that God is talking about the natural Jewish descendants of Abraham.

> *And they also, if they do not continue in unbelief, will be grafted in, for God is able to graft them in again. For if you were cut out of the olive tree which is wild by nature, and were grafted contrary to nature into a good olive tree, how much more will these, who are the natural branches, be grafted into their own olive tree? For I do not desire, brethren, that you should be ignorant of this mystery, lest you should be wise in your own opinion, that hardening in part has happened to Israel until the fullness of the*

Gentiles has come in. And so all Israel will be saved, as it is written: "The Deliverer will come out of Zion, and He will turn away ungodliness from Jacob; for this is my covenant with them, when I take away their sins." Concerning the gospel they are enemies for your sake, but concerning the election they are beloved for the sake of the fathers. For the gifts and the calling of God are irrevocable (Romans 11:23-29).

The last verse, the great promise about God's gifts and calling being irrevocable, has been preached by many over the centuries and has been applied to a host of different situations: personal, family, church, denominational, and even national. However, the literal textual application of verse 29 is specifically applied to natural Israel. God has *not* permanently divorced her. She is destined to be forgiven and restored!

Why Does It Matter to Us?

Let us turn now to the third and final question. Why would the doctrine of the permanent rejection of national Israel threaten the Church? If God said He would keep His covenant to a thousand generations, (which He did in Psalm 105:7-11), then how good is God's word? If God could give promises to Israel and break them, then why should we be confident that He will keep His word to us? The very doctrine of the nature of God is at stake. Some may say, "But, Jesus died for us and the Holy Spirit has sealed our salvation!" Of course this is true, but we know it and accept it by *faith*. What if God decided to change

His mind? Could we appeal to Him to keep His word based on *our* character or works? Certainly not! For that matter, who could appeal to a God who could not be trusted?

Do you see how unfounded and dangerous it is to suggest that God broke His covenant with Israel? God's very essence is that of a covenant keeper. He is the ultimate Promise Keeper. It is man who cannot be trusted:

> ...*Let God be true but every man a liar (Romans 3:4).*

Let us pray for the people of Israel that God would forgive their sins, open their eyes to Messiah Jesus, and totally restore them to their land and their God! Isaiah predicts the coming of Jesus as Messiah in Isaiah 11:10; in verse 11 He says that YAHWEH shall bring back Israel "the second time" and in verse 12 He says:

> *He will set up a banner for the nations, And will assemble the outcasts of Israel, And gather together the dispersed of Judah From the four corners of the earth!*

This is now being fulfilled. Praise the Lord Jesus!

In Ezekiel's vision of the dry bones in chapter 37, he saw the bones come together *before* they received their life-breath. Israel is now being gathered as dry bones. Today's question is the same: "Can these bones live?" It is my deep conviction that we are living in the generation of the salvation of Israel. It has begun! Many stories have been told in detail of the amazing experiences regarding the exodus of Jews from Russia and the rest of the former Soviet Union as well as from over 160 other nations. The bones are coming together.

If God supernaturally reveals Jesus as Messiah to Israel in these last days, what is the Church going to do? The answer is in the wisdom of Acts 15 where the council wrestled with *the Gentile problem.* What were they going to do about Gentiles being saved? Did they need to be *Judaized?* You see, most believers then were Jews. The answer was a clear *no.* It was enough that they receive Jesus, avoid immorality, and abstain from idols. Today, almost all believers are formerly Gentile and we are seeing the *same problem in reverse.* As more Jews are saved, we will have to face the question: Do Jews need to be *gentilized* and become culturally Gentile in order to be saved? The wise answer once again is *no.* It is enough that they receive Jesus as Messiah. They are *not pagans,* in the classic sense, if they worship the God of Abraham, Isaac, and Jacob. They do not need to renounce their God and convert to a "Christian God," but they do need to recognize that dependence upon the law is not a means of salvation. All who are saved in both Testaments are saved by faith as Abraham...

did not waver at the promise of God through unbelief, but was strengthened in faith, giving glory to God, and being fully convinced that what He had promised He was also able to perform. And therefore "it was accounted to him for righteousness" (Romans 4:20-22). And he believed in YAHWEH and He accounted it to him for righteousness" (Genesis 15:6).

Faith believes YAHWEH. He is the only God and Jesus is His Messiah. *Jews do not need to renounce Judaism, but they must accept Jesus,* Who said:

> *I am the way, the truth, and the life. No man comes to the Father except through Me* (John 14:6).

If you, dear reader, have not been saved, you simply need to turn from your sin and believe God's promise of forgiveness through Jesus (Yeshua) the Messiah. It is God Who saves.

> *For by grace you have been saved through faith, and that not of yourselves; it is the gift of God, not of works, lest anyone should boast* (Eph. 2:8-9).

Why not talk to God yourself right now and settle this issue in your life for all eternity?

GOD IS FAITHFUL!

Chapter 11

Overcoming Replacement Theology

Replacement theology...divorces God from His own character

The above statement frames the entire case against replacement theology. For God to replace Israel with a completely new entity for His grace is to violate the nature of God. If all His promises were conditional upon man's behavior, you might have an argument. However, some of His promises are unconditional and therefore rest only on His immutable character and word. Therefore, since He cannot lie, Israel is redeemed in the end.

> *For I am YAHWEH, I do not change; Therefore you are not consumed, O sons of Jacob* (Malachi 3:6). *Jesus Christ is the same yesterday, today, and forever* (Hebrews 13:8).

If God changes, Jacob disappears. They deserve it, but they have not disappeared, because He keeps His word to their fathers: Abraham, Isaac and Jacob. YAHWEH is the ultimate promise keeper.

Yet, replacement theology, **RT**, is in the DNA of the Church. **RT** has prevailed so long that Christians assume it. How do we overcome such ingrained thinking? Look at the character of God and the testimony of history. The testimony of God's heart and words is one side of the coin. The other is the testimony of history through the prophets, the apostles and the actual historical events. Overcoming the numbing effect of replacement theology is not only possible, it is critical.

Testimony of History

This quotation is from my good friend John Fisk.

There has never been a group of people or a nation which has endured such persecution and maintained their identity. Again and again this people, who had no land, no allies, and no apparent reason to exist; endured. Even more astounding, is that few have recognized these historical anomalies. God said He would scatter His people to every nation. They were still identifiable in every nation after 1,900 years of wandering, 1,900 years of persecution, and 1,900 years of exile from their own land. Few noticed. He said He would bring them back. He did! Few noticed. The probability of this must be in the stratosphere. When you consider that for the entire 1,900 years the Jews were never accepted by any of the nations into which they were scattered. At every turn, Satan used all the forces at his disposal to destroy this people of God and could not. This was so pervasive, that special words such as Holocaust, pogroms or anti-Semitism invaded the language and few noticed. Indeed, I have often heard some say: "The Jews are just like any other people." Rather than recognize the events that surround this people, as God's divine providence on His chosen people, the Church has chosen instead to fight the people of God.

One point that bears repeating is that you could make a pretty good case against the restoration of Israel before 1948. Since then, however, it becomes harder as events overtake theology. Israel became a modern nation recognized by the United Nations. She won several wars and regained sovereignty over ancient Jerusalem, naming it as the capital city. Millions of Jews have now returned to Israel, coming from virtually every nation on earth. Even the rise of Islam fits into the exact Bible prophecies that were spiritualized in the past. Now, we see these literal promises miraculously fulfilled in one generation.

The Awakening

It is time for the Church to wake up, not only to our Hebrew roots, but to the proactive purpose of God in these last days. **RT** is like a disease in the blood. We former gentiles were saved and added to the Kingdom by a spiritual blood transfusion from Jesus, the Jewish Messiah. We welcome forgiveness of our sins and eternal life, but we don't like His family lineage. Yet, we get the whole package when we get Jesus. The sooner we embrace our new adopted family the better.

Disclaimer

Rabbinic Judaism is not the same as scriptural Judaism. Over 200 years before the Messiah came; the rabbis started embracing the idea of two Torahs, the written Hebrew text plus *oral tradition*. This oral law was exalted to be equal to or even transcend scripture. This opened the door for private interpretations by many scholar rabbis that were held to be equal to, or higher than the scripture itself. This same error was repeated by Christendom beginning just a couple hundred years after Jesus, and continuing to this present day. This great error is called *traditions of men*. Both Jews and Christians have been guilty of this error. Jesus blasted the Pharisees for this hypocrisy.

> *He answered and said to them, "Why do you also transgress the commandment of God because of your tradition? For God commanded, saying, 'Honor your father and your mother'; and, 'He who curses father or mother, let him be put to death.' But you say, 'Whoever says to his father or mother, "Whatever profit you might have received from me is a gift to God"-- then he need not honor his father or mother.' Thus you have made the commandment of God of no effect by your tradition. Hypocrites! Well did Isaiah prophesy about you, saying: 'These*

people draw near to Me with their mouth, And honor Me with their lips, But their heart is far from Me. And in vain they worship Me, Teaching as doctrines the commandments of men (Matthew 15:3-9).

I stand for the restoration of Biblical Judaism in contrast with Rabbinic. In the same way, I stand for Biblical restoration of modern Israel which often conflicts with decisions of the present Israeli government.

One New Man

So then, how do we overcome **RT**? Rather than launching a counter offensive to refute it, I propose we keep our eye on the goal. The end game of God's strategy for His community of believers is declared in Ephesians 2. It is called *one new man*. All the former gentiles who follow Jesus are grafted into the commonwealth of Israel.

Therefore remember that you, once Gentiles in the flesh--who are called Uncircumcision by what is called the Circumcision made in the flesh by hands-- that at that time you were without Christ, being aliens from the commonwealth of Israel and strangers from the covenants of promise, having no hope and without God in the world. But now in Christ Jesus you who once were far off have been brought near by the blood of Christ. For He Himself is our peace, who has made both one, and has broken down the middle wall of separation, having abolished in

His flesh the enmity, that is, the law of commandments contained in ordinances, so as to create in Himself one new man from the two, thus making peace, (Ephesians 2:11-15).

We will overcome **RT** therefore, not by convincing all Christendom of our theology, but by yielding to the facts on the ground. It will be settled by history and by separation. True believers in the literal message of the Bible will gravitate toward the inevitable victory. The rest will be caught in the great deception and delusion of which Paul warned, and find themselves on the outside of God's plan.

And then the lawless one will be revealed, whom the Lord will consume with the breath of His mouth and destroy with the brightness of His coming. The coming of the lawless one is according to the working of Satan, with all power, signs, and lying wonders, and with all unrighteous deception among those who perish, because they did not receive the love of the truth, that they might be saved. And for this reason God will send them strong delusion, that they should believe the lie, (2 Thessalonians 2:8-11).

Replacement theology, **RT**, is a lie.

The Great Coming Merger

For many years I faithfully taught that Israel and the Church were on parallel tracks of prophecy. A few years ago, the Holy Spirit corrected me. Although they have indeed been on separate tracks historically, they are not parallel, they are **merging.** This is impossible in the natural. There is too much history between the two, too much bad blood. However, when God say He will do something, nothing is impossible with Him. How He will do it, or when He will do it, is still a mystery. But the merger is coming, and soon. Jews and Christians are destined to be reconciled into *one new man.*

No Longer Gentile

One final point can be made to add clarification to this subject. A case can be made that the Biblical usage of the term *gentile,* refers to any people or nations who do not know God. Indeed, the apostle Paul reveals a little recognized fact in several of his letters. Note the tense emphasized in the following quotes.

> *Therefore remember that you,* **once** *Gentiles in the flesh--who are called Uncircumcision by what is called the Circumcision made in the flesh by hands--that* **at that time you were without Christ, being aliens** *from the commonwealth of Israel and strangers from the covenants of promise, having no hope and without God in the world* **But now** *in Christ Jesus you who once were far off have been brought near by the blood of Christ* (Ephesians 2:11-13).

This indicates that Paul viewed the condition of the Ephesian believers to have changed. These had been worshippers of the Greek goddess, Diana. They were previously gentiles and aliens from the commonwealth of Israel but are now citizens of Israel through Jesus.

Here is another example in Paul's letter to the Corinthian church, whose identification as *gentiles* is in the past tense.

*You know that you **were** Gentiles, carried away to these dumb idols; however you were led* (1 Corinthians 12:2).

In both of these examples the Greek word for gentiles is *ethnos* from which we get our English word *ethnic*. My conclusion, therefore, is that when a gentile who does not know the God of Israel gets saved, he becomes a citizen of Israel. I know that today's political nation of Israel does not see it that way, but God does. Also, it is important to note that when a Jew accepts that Jesus is the son of God and Messiah, he is not converting to a Christian God. Rather, we who **were once** gentiles have converted to YAHWEH, the God of Abraham, Isaac, and Jacob. We think we are converting to Jesus, but He always maintained that He was reconciling us to the Father. We are really converting from our paganism or atheism or secular humanism to the living Creator God! We worship the God of Israel, and the Messiah King of Israel. When He returns, our ultimate capital city is not going to be Rome or Washington or Brussels or Mecca. Our predestined capital is Jerusalem, Israel.

GOD IS FAITHFUL!

Chapter 12

Three Unfulfilled Prophecies

It stands to reason that if we are indeed living in the last generation of this age, there will be Bible prophecies fulfilled right before our eyes. Many Christians expect the antichrist to appear and enforce the New World Order. Much has been written on the subject. However, we will zero in on three specific unfulfilled prophecies that happen **before** Armageddon and the final battles.

First, this chapter details Bible prophecy that is now happening in Gaza. Secondly, in Chapter 13, we look at a major disaster about to occur, the destruction of Damascus, Syria's capital city. The third unfulfilled prophecy is the Psalm 83 War, explained in depth, also in Chapter 13.

Everyone wants to know about the Second Coming and the antichrist, but pertinent scriptures about Gaza need to be considered first. We are still living in Bible times. No more books will be added to the Bible, but many last days prophecies are being fulfilled right before our eyes. It is exciting to see these Biblical mileposts passing by us every day. Some Christians focus on the *thief in the night* concept without making the critical distinction between believers and unbelievers. It is the unbelievers who will be surprised by the sudden appearing of Messiah Jesus. Believers are children of the light and will not be surprised.

> *But you brethren are not in darkness, so that this Day should overtake you as a thief (I* Thessalonians 5:4).

This study is designed to provoke a deeper look at Gaza in the Bible. This tiny strip of land on Israel's southern coastline has been moving up the list of God's datelines. Are you aware that the Bible predicts that Gaza will be destroyed by fire?

Gaza on Fire

> *Thus says YAHWEH: For three transgressions of Gaza, and for four, I will not turn away its punishment, Because they took captive the whole captivity To deliver them up to Edom. But I will send a* **fire upon the wall of Gaza,** *Which shall devour its palaces.* (Amos 1:6-7).

When Gaza was separated from Egypt and identified as a separate territory occupied by Israel in 1967, a situation existed which only the Israeli prophets of old had foreseen. What they had to say about Gaza, would unfold 2,500 years after the words were penned. Gaza did not have a wall historically until the present day and has never been destroyed by fire. Therefore, it must still be in the future.

In recent history, Gaza was controlled by Britain under the British Mandate till Egypt took it over after the 1948 War of Israeli Independence. Israel took Gaza in the 1967 Six Day War. In August of 2005, Israel withdrew all 10,000 of the Jewish residents, under United States and international pressure. Hamas took over Gaza from the Palestinian Authority, in June of 2007 leading to the present chaos.

You can see five stages of Gaza's judgment predicted in Bible prophecy:

1. A wall is built around Gaza.

2. Israel withdraws from Gaza.

3. Chaos overtakes Gaza. Anarchy reigns.

4. Gaza is destroyed by fire.

5. Israel returns to inhabit Gaza.

Now, let's look at each of these stages individually.

1. The Gaza Wall

The wall was built just a few years ago between Gaza and Israel and between Gaza and Egypt. It has become infamous. Palestinians have dug smuggling tunnels under it, shot rockets over it, and generally have done everything in their power to circumvent it. There is great irony in the fact that they do not dig tunnels to escape Gaza but to import weapons to kill Israelis.

For the fulfillment of the *fire on the wall* scripture, Gaza must exist and have a wall.   Gaza is an identifiable political entity.   So, only now can the scripture in Amos 1:7 be fulfilled. The wall is complete.

2. Israel Withdraws from Gaza

All the Jews were forcibly removed from Gaza in August of 2005. This had seemed unthinkable, given that Ariel Sharon, father of the settlement movement, was Prime Minister of Israel. Jews had lived and prospered in Gaza for 100 years. But, under tremendous pressure from the United States and the international community, Israel yielded yet again, to the seductive false peace.

The agriculture from Gaza comprised 15% of Israel's agricultural exports.   However, the buildings and large green houses that they left behind were destroyed by the Palestinians. The economy of Gaza fell into an abyss, with 50% unemployment. The Gaza Palestinians invited every terrorist group on the planet to come and establish their headquarters there in Gaza.

Those who know their God are completely opposed to Israel giving up any of the land, but God has a prophetic revelation about Gaza and Israel's 2005 withdrawal. We see a definite prophetic Biblical plan. However, we do not find similar texts indicating withdrawal from Judea and Samaria (the West Bank). The tragedy of Sharon's Disengagement Plan was compounded soon after the evacuation when the old war hero fell victim to a massive stroke that left him in a coma for more than four years.

Parallel Judgments

Some observers have pointed out a trend, that the United States suffered consequences each time we opposed God's purpose for Israel. This is particularly evident with Gaza. We exerted unprecedented pressure on the Sharon government to unilaterally leave Gaza. Even as Israel began the withdrawal, Hurricane Katrina formed in the Atlantic and resulted in a devastating blow to New Orleans. It has been calculated that the percentage of the total population of Israel evacuated from Gaza, is the precise percentage of the US population that was evacuated from New Orleans. I highly recommend an excellent book on the subject of the cause and effect of United States actions against Israel entitled: Eye To Eye, by White House Correspondent William Koenig.[7]

2009 brought major changes for Israel with Prime Minister Benjamin Netanyahu declaring "No Shortcuts" to peace. Meanwhile, President Obama continued to push the failed two-state "Road Map" process, making demands only of Israel. This U.S. interference met increased resistance from P.M. Netanyahu and Israel's new government. The whole Middle East has coalesced into the prophetic picture painted so clearly by the scriptures.

For behold, in those days and at that time, When
I bring back the captives of Judah and

---

[7] William Koenig, *Eye to Eye*, Alexandria, Virginia by About Him Publishing

*Jerusalem, I will also gather all nations, And bring them down to the Valley of Jehoshaphat; And I will enter into judgment with them there On account of My people, My heritage Israel, Whom they have scattered among the nations; They have also **divided up My land**   (Joel 3:1-2).*

God will judge the nations because they divided His land. The *two state plan* is dividing God's land.

Israel's unilateral withdrawal from Gaza in August 2005 was primary in prophetic events that are still playing out. Look at the Gaza withdrawal disaster related to the United States position. We are so blessed as a country. But does that mean we get a free pass when God starts judging the world? Remember the warning to Esther not to think that just because she lived in the King's house that she would be spared the terrible events about to happen. Our prosperity and blessing places us in the exact dilemma that Esther faced. We should heed the same warning applied to America, the "King's House". Our blessed standing in the world is only by the mercy of God.

Remember God's promise to Abraham:

I will make you a great nation; I will bless you and make your name great; and you shall be a blessing. I will bless those who bless you, and I will curse him who curses you; and in you all the families of the earth shall be blessed (Genesis 12:2-3).

Every nation, every family, and every person will be judged accordingly. Jerusalem's peace is Yahweh's highest priority. Therefore, we must pray fervently for the peace of Jerusalem. Pray that Israel turns away from her suitors and looks to YAHWEH for salvation. There is terrific pressure on Israel to look to the United States for her salvation. But no other nation will save Israel, only the Messiah can do that. Don't think it is a coincidence that we are the only superpower and that we are pro-Israel. If the United States forsakes Israel, we will fall from our blessed position overnight. Pray!

An important key to understanding Gaza is given in Zephaniah.

> *Before the decree is issued, Or the day passes like chaff, Before YAHWEH'S fierce anger comes upon you, Before the day of YAHWEH'S anger comes upon you! Seek YAHWEH, all you meek of the earth, Who have upheld His justice. Seek righteousness, seek humility. It may be that you will be hidden In the day of YAHWEH'S anger. For* **Gaza shall be forsaken** (Zephaniah 2:2-4a).

The timing of this prophecy is clear in verses 2 and 3, as *the day of YAHWEH'S anger.* I have often proposed a response to the New Age bumper sticker: *Visualize World Peace.* My alternative bumper sticker is: *Visualize the Wrath of God!* This is not a mean spirited or fleshly idea, but rather the real order of things. Before we see true world peace, we will first see the judgment of God against violence and evil. Israel will only know true peace when they recognize that Jesus, Prince of Peace (Yeshua Sar Shalom) is the only One Who will bring peace. National Israel will ultimately recognize Him and say: *Baruch ha ba ha Shem Adonai! (YAHWEH) - Blessed is He who comes in the name of the LORD (YAHWEH).* It is my strong conviction that they will actually use His real name, as documented earlier in this book. Bible students know that the ultimate end of evil through God's wrath is great news. God's justice in the final elimination of evil is the *other half* of the Gospel. Romans 1:16-18 speaks of the revelation of both the righteousness of God, and the wrath of God.

3. Chaos and Anarchy

Now, let's go back to Zephaniah for a revelation of the spiritual principality that rules Gaza. What led to the anarchy and chaos that prevails in Gaza, especially since Hamas threw out the Palestinian Authority in 2007?

> *Woe to the inhabitants of the seacoast, The nation of the Cherethites! The word of YAHWEH is against you, O Canaan, land of the Philistines: I will destroy you; So there shall be no inhabitant* (Zephaniah 2:5).

This verse identifies Gazans, as *Cherethites,* or literally in the Hebrew text: *Assassins!* It would seem to be a simple step to understanding this reference as an ancient way of describing the *suicide/homicide bombers* of today! Sheikh Ahmed Ismail Hassan Yassin was the father of suicide bombing and, with Abdel Aziz al-Rantisi, were the cofounders of the Hamas movement. Yassin and Rantisi were killed in 2004 within one month of each other. Were their deaths prophesied? Was the death of Yassar Arafat part of God's final judgment on Gaza? Arafat also cleverly used this suicide weapon, but kept it at arm's length. His death cleared the way for Gaza's judgment. His current replacement, Mahmoud Abbas, aka Abu Mazen, along with Hamas, may face the same justice of Zechariah 9:4-6, which says *the king shall perish* from Gaza. Why is there anarchy under Hamas? There will be no king or authority in Gaza!

> *Ashkelon shall see it and fear; Gaza also shall be very sorrowful; And Ekron, for He dried up her expectation.* **The king shall perish from Gaza,** *And Ashkelon shall not be inhabited* (Zechariah 9:5).

You may already know that the Gaza based terrorist group Hamas is named from an Arabic acronym that forms the word pronounced *hamas* in English. What you may not know is that hamas is actually a real Hebrew word used in the Bible. It means *violence.* It is precisely the word used in Genesis 6:11 & 13 describing the violence in the earth that offended God. The acronym was chosen to intimidate Hebrew speaking Israelis. The literal translation of Hamas in English is Violence, the exact thing that brought Noah's flood. The political correctness obsession of Western nations purposely obfuscates the sharper definition of our true enemy. (Obfuscate means to confuse, make unclear or to darken.) It has become politically incorrect to exactly translate certain Arabic words, so as not to offend Muslims. Another example is our Western insistence on translating the war cry of *Allahu Akhbar* simply as God is great. They are not saying God (YAHWEH) is great. They are saying Allah is greater! Don't be deceived by this obfuscation. The god of Islam is not the same as our Father God. Allah is not a father. A billion and a half Muslims of Islam are in bondage to a pagan Arabian deity called Allah and a false Jesus called Isa who did not die on the cross for our sins, according to Muslim theology. Islam and the Koran adamantly teach that Allah has no son, in irreconcilable contradiction to the Bible. Consider even this Old Testament question:

> *Who has ascended into heaven, or descended? Who has gathered the wind in His fists? Who has bound the waters in a garment? Who has established all the ends of the earth? What is His name, and what is His Son's name, If you know?* (Proverbs 30:4).

We worship God and Jesus the Son of God (in Hebrew: Yahweh and Yeshua Ben Yahweh). There is abundant historical background to support this point. Muslims trace their genealogy through Abraham and Ishmael. The Judeo Christian heritage follows the God of Abraham, Isaac and Jacob. The Bible unquestionably traces the blessings of God through Jacob/Israel. We are witnessing millions of former Muslims who have turned from a false Jesus to the Jesus of the Bible as the Son of God who is the true Messiah for Israel and all who trust in His mercy. We pray for the salvation of Arabs as well as Jews.

(Reminder note: The Hebrew text clearly uses the personal name for God, YAHWEH. Therefore, I am on a mission to see His name used comfortably again. This is especially necessary in the context of the rise of the Islamic pagan god which commands the use of that personal name. I don't insist on overuse of YAHWEH, but it is time to restore His wonderful and Almighty Name.)

4. Fire on the Wall

The five stages of Gaza's judgment have reached Stage Four—Destruction. Operation Cast Lead, by Israel in January 2009, was the beginning of the end for Gaza. At last report there are less than 400 born again Christians in Gaza and no Jews. When they escape or die, will Gaza be destroyed like Sodom and Gomorrah? Gaza is teetering on the brink of disaster. Consider this.

> *Woe to the inhabitants of the seacoast, The nation of the Cherethites! The word of YAHWEH is against you, O Canaan, land of the Philistines: I will destroy you; So there shall be* **no inhabitant** (Zephaniah 2:5).

Wow! Can that possibly mean what it says? Was God behind evacuating the Jews because He is about to bring a devastating judgment on Gaza? Could He be sparing these Jews the forth coming Gaza judgment? The Gaza War in January 2009 had "fire on the wall" just as in:

Thus says YAHWEH: For three transgressions of Gaza, and for four, I will not turn away its punishment, Because they took captive the whole captivity To deliver them up to Edom. But I will send a fire upon the wall of Gaza, Which shall devour its palaces (Amos 1:6-7).

Video footage of forty foot walls of fire were broadcast around the world! There wasn't even a wall around Gaza in history until Israel built it in 1994 and 2004.

5. Israel Returns to Gaza

The seacoast shall be pastures, With shelters for shepherds and folds for flocks. The coast shall be for the remnant of the house of Judah; They shall feed their flocks there; In the houses of Ashkelon they shall lie down at evening. For YAHWEH their God will intervene for them, And return their captives (Zephaniah 2:6-7).

Finally, Zephaniah pictures Gaza after the judgment as a place where shepherds tend their sheep and a place for the remnant of the house of Judah. Israel will return. How will this happen? When will it happen? Stay tuned to the Holy Spirit yourself, as you study these important passages. The more we see Hamas dominating Gaza, the closer we get to the restoration of Gaza to Israel. In 2008, Hamas blew up the wall facing Egypt and a half million Gazans flooded into Egypt for a few days. Gaza is teetering on the brink of disaster. In the end Israel will possess all of the Land God has promised. It will not matter even if all the nations of the earth are opposed, as declared in Psalm 2. Pray for the peace of Jerusalem!

GOD IS FAITHFUL!

Chapter 13

Damascus and the Psalm 83 War

Gaza was the first of three unfulfilled prophecies that are now coming to pass. This chapter deals with two others that are imminent. Isaiah saw a very dark vision of Damascus that has not happened yet in history. We will also consider a prophesied war that has yet to happen, found in Psalm 83. But first, let's set the stage.

Jerusalem the Prize

By 2010 Jerusalem had emerged as a primary focus of world attention, just as Zechariah boldly predicted over 2,500 years ago, by the inspiration of the Holy Spirit.

Behold, I will make Jerusalem a cup of drunkenness to all the surrounding peoples, when they lay siege against Judah and Jerusalem And it shall happen in that day that I will make Jerusalem a very heavy stone for all peoples; all who would heave it away will surely be cut in pieces, though all nations of the earth are gathered against it (Zechariah 12:2-3).

God's heart is toward Jerusalem. His promises are being kept.

Behold, He who keeps Israel Shall neither slumber nor sleep (Psalm 121:4).

We often take requests in our prayer meetings and I like to point out that God has His own prayer request:

Pray for the peace of Jerusalem: May they prosper who love you. (Psalm 122:6)

My friend John Fisk observes that *Jerusalem is not the target, it is the prize.* The whole world is taking sides with the Palestinians to divide the city and make the eastern half the capital of a Palestinian state. This ignores the historic reality that there has never been a state called Palestine. Furthermore, Jerusalem has never been the capital city of any other country in history, only Israel. King David made Jerusalem the capital of Israel over 3,000 years ago. Nevertheless, the battle lines are now being drawn over Jerusalem and the Temple Mount. Before the final battle of Armageddon, there are three preliminary events prophesied. They may occur separately, but more likely, at the same time. We have looked at Gaza; now let's turn our attention to Damascus and the Psalm 83 War.

Damascus Destroyed

There are many prophecies yet to be fulfilled before the Second Coming of Jesus. However, few are as ominous and certain as this remarkable text from the book of Isaiah.

> ... *burden against Damascus. "Behold, Damascus will cease from being a city, And it will be a ruinous heap"* ....*Then behold, at eventide, trouble! And before the morning, he is no more. This is the portion of those who plunder us, And the lot of those who rob us* (Isaiah 17:1 & 14).

This quote is the first verse and the last verse from Isaiah 17. The passage between these verses deals with a broader picture than I will cover here. But, what do we do about the clear declaration that Damascus *will cease from being a city?* This amazing prophecy must be taken literally. It speaks of the city left as a pile of rubble.

History gives us a profound fact. All of the major Middle East capital cities have been destroyed at various times in history. Jerusalem, for example, has been destroyed at least eleven times. The one exception to this is Damascus. It lays claim to being one of the oldest continuously inhabited cities on earth, if not the very oldest. Yet, with all of the swirling wars, throughout ancient times and modern, Damascus has never been destroyed.

Some prophecies can have dual fulfillment in ancient and modern times. This one in Isaiah 17:1, however, has only one literal fulfillment: future. Therefore, since we are in the last generation, Damascus' days are numbered. A literal fulfillment would have to be very soon. Watching developments in Syria certainly leads one to allow that it could indeed be close.

Syria has entered into a treaty with Iran, and the two are patrons of Lebanon and Hezbollah. Evidence of chemical WMD (weapons of mass destruction) have been found in the possession of Syria. Many Iranians and Syrians were killed when an accident occurred in Syria, while staging a missile with a chemical warhead on July 26, 2007. An on going clandestine nuclear program in Syria was given little notice, even when Israel bombed and destroyed Syrian nuclear facilities September 6, 2007. Recent new alliances have been formed with Iran and Turkey changing the balance of power in the region. Israel cannot stand by and allow her own extinction. All of this fits in quite well with the Psalm 83 War scenario dealt with next.

There is another clue regarding the destruction of Damascus in the last verse of Isaiah 17.

> *Then behold, at eventide, trouble! And before the morning, he is no more. This is the portion of those who plunder us, And the lot of those who rob us* (Isaiah 17:14).

This suggests that there could be a warning of some sort the night before and then the calamity before morning. This is consistent with Israel's method of warning civilians before striking militarily. In the 2009 Gaza War, Israel made hundreds of thousands of cell phone calls announcing where they would be bombing, so civilians could flee. They also dropped leaflets with the warnings. They did this also in the 2006 Second Lebanon War.

We do not know how Isaiah 17 will be fulfilled, but we know Damascus will be destroyed, and quite likely, very soon. Perhaps it will happen, along with Gaza, in the war predicted in Psalm 83. All three of these specific prophetic events could happen at the same time.

Israel's Next Regional War

The war described in this Psalm is quite unusual compared to Israel's other modern wars. In each previous case, all the adjacent countries attacked Israel. In Psalm 83, oddly, Egypt is not mentioned. Therefore, it is logical to conclude that a regional war is still coming that excludes Egypt. Currently, the only two Arab or Muslim states that have peace treaties with Israel are Egypt and Jordan. It stands to reason that Egypt would sit out the next war, but what about Jordan?

Jordan is clearly included in Psalm 83, so I predict a major change in Jordanian politics resulting in Jordan falling into the Iranian/Syrian camp. It is estimated that up to 65 per cent of their population is Palestinian. Only a small minority is actually part of King Abdullah's Hashemite family line of the monarchy. So, the King will either turn against Israel, or be removed and the monarchy overthrown. It could be from abdication, exile or even worse; but it will occur in order for Psalm 83 to be fulfilled. There are major shifts already in Jordan and it could happen before this book is printed.

The Second Lebanon War in the summer of 2006 was the beginning of the Psalm 83 War. Even now Lebanon has effectively fallen into Hezbollah control which aligns Lebanon with Iran, since Hezbollah is Iran's proxy. Hamas in Gaza is also backed and supplied by Iran. So, the stage is set, and all that remains is for Jordan to fall into place.

Digging In

We need to examine the context of the next war in light of the details of Psalm 83. It would be good to read the entire Psalm at this point. I will only highlight certain parts. There are several sections, each progressing to the conclusion of a victory for Israel. It starts with why the enemies of Israel attack, and reveals in order: **motive, goal, method, participants, prayer and result.**

> *For behold, Your enemies make a tumult; And those who hate You have lifted up their head. They have taken crafty counsel against Your people, And consulted together against Your sheltered ones. They have said, "Come, and let us cut them off from being a nation, That the name of Israel may be remembered no more. For they have consulted together with one consent; They form a confederacy against You* (Psalm 83:2-5).

Their **motive** is hatred of God (YAHWEH). They can't get to Him directly, so through *crafty counsel*, they decide to attack His beloved nation. Their **goal** is to so completely destroy them, that the very name *Israel* is forgotten in world history. Their **method** is to form a confederacy which indicates multiple countries and groups with mixed background, but a unified purpose: the destruction of Israel.

The Name

This issue of wiping out the name of Israel is no small thing. Even today, Israel's enemies refuse to say the name. They refer to the *Zionist entity,* or the *occupiers,* or simply *Zionists,* but will not use the name, Israel. This obsession is directly related to their hatred of God and the exalting of the god of Islam over YAHWEH, the God Abraham, Isaac and Jacob, the God of Israel. The ultimate goal is the defeat of YAHWEH and the blocking out of His name. This was covered in chapters 4-6 of my book, explaining the restoration of the name of YAHWEH.

Psalm 83:6-8 lists the **participants** in this war. It includes all the countries around Israel with the notable exception of Egypt. Iraq may be interpreted to be in the list which would indicate some change in direction for the current government of Iraq. Saudi Arabia also appears to be included in the list. Perhaps these last two countries are in a support role more than an overt one. Remember that the confederacy involves some cunning and deception.

> *Deal with them as with Midian, As with Sisera, As with Jabin at the Brook Kishon, Who perished at En Dor, Who became as refuse on the earth. Make their nobles like Oreb and like Zeeb, Yes, all their princes like Zebah and Zalmunna Who*

said, "Let us take for ourselves The pastures of God for a possession" (Psalm 83:9-12).

This **prayer** of the Psalmist, Asaph, reminds God of His past victories for Israel. The victory of Gideon over Oreb and Zeeb, the two princes of the Midianites in Judges 7, was followed by the capture and execution of the Midianite kings, Zebah and Zalmunna in Judges 8. An interesting side note here is that after Gideon killed them, he *took the crescent ornaments that were on their camel's necks* (Judges 8:21). This confirms that they were moon worshippers, an ancient predecessor to modern Islam.

Fill their faces with shame, That they may seek Your name, O YAHWEH. Let them be confounded and dismayed forever; Yes, let them be put to shame and perish That they may know that You, whose name alone is YAHWEH, Are the Most High over all the earth (Psalm 83:16-18).

The **result** of the prayer is God's victory for Israel, but also something more. Asaph asks God that the enemies become ashamed and seek the face of YAHWEH. This seems to indicate an opportunity for them to turn to God, but also includes perishing eternally if they refuse to repent. Either way, they will know that the God, whose name is YAHWEH, is the supreme God of the whole earth. In light of such strong last day prophecy about using and acknowledging His name, how can we ignore this rising emphasis on knowing the personal name of YAHWEH? Perhaps the Psalm 83 war will signal the public awakening to the fact that the Creator God of the universe and the Bible has a personal name distinct from all other gods of man. Pray for the peace of Jerusalem!

GOD IS FAITHFUL!

Chapter 14

The Glory of God

People ask if it will get better and better, or worse and worse, until Jesus comes. The answer is yes. It will get better for believers, and worse for the ungodly. God will judge the wicked in the end; and in one sense, that is certainly good news. Yet, there is much better news for believers. We will not sit this one out, watching from the sidelines. More than any previous time in history, God's people will play a major role in the last day heroics. If there were to be a third testament, it would record the saints and heroes of the faith of our day, just like Hebrews 11, the hall of fame of faith.

Our study of the last generation concludes at the highest point. God extends His glory to His people, so that His finest hour becomes our finest hour. We started with the metaphor of the Red Sea sun resurrected out of the ocean like Israel rose out of the sea of nations in our time. In the same way, like a sunrise, YAHWEH'S glory will rise upon His people in a spectacular empowerment for believers to finally rise up and shine in the face of terrible darkness in the earth.

My wife Doreen, and I were commissioned as missionaries in 1968 after a seven and a half month post graduate missionary internship training program. The commissioning banquet had a profound theme: *Candles Are for Dark Places*. It has influenced our lives throughout the years since. Yet, it was only in recent years that I have begun to catch a glimpse of the magnitude of God's purpose and timing to share His glory, to literally put His glory on us. He intends for us to be sources of light for the lost. We are not to be like a moon reflecting the glory of the sun. We are to shine like the sun because the glory of God is in us. We will shine like the sun because we live in the Son, Jesus, and He lives in us.

Isaiah 60 contains a hidden revelation that is opening up now, because it is time for its fulfillment. Proverbs 25:2 talks about it being God's glory to hide a matter, and our glory to search it out. Let us search for that which is hidden in Isaiah 60. There are several key verses and points of emphasis. We have already discovered the amazing revelation in the Psalm 102:18 original Hebrew text, confirming that we are the generation LAST. This Isaiah passage also has a surprise in the original Hebrew text.

> *Arise; shine; For your light has come! And the glory of YAHWEH is risen upon you. For behold, the darkness shall cover the earth, And deep darkness the people; But YAHWEH will arise over*

you, And His glory will be seen upon you. The
Gentiles shall come to your light, And kings to
the brightness of your rising. Lift up your eyes all
around, and see: They all gather together, they
come to you; Your sons shall come from afar,
And your daughters shall be nursed at your side.
Then you shall see and become radiant, And
your heart shall swell with joy; Because the
abundance of the sea shall be turned to you,
The wealth of the Gentiles shall come to you.

Radiant!

More than a dozen words in this passage speak of
light, shining, brightness, rising, see, be seen, radiant and
similar language that all relates to something quite
visible. These words all describe the effect of God's glory
on us. We do not reflect His glory, He gives us His glory.
It **radiates** from us. This stretches our faith at first. We
have been so indoctrinated that only God has the glory.
Our ignorance leads to a false humility at the point of this
critical revelation.

This confusion is influenced by a mistaken
interpretation of another verse.

I am YAHWEH, that is My name; And My glory I
*will not give to **another,** Nor My praise to*
carved images (Isaiah 42:8).

This is usually explained as saying God will not give His
glory to anyone else. Yet, Isaiah 60 clearly says He will
put His glory on us. This appears to be a contradiction,

but there is no contradiction if you understand the context of 42:8. God will not give His glory to **other gods or idols.** This then leaves open the possibility for God to put His glory on His people.

Also, notice the fact that the personal pronoun *you or yours* is used fifteen times in our quote from Isaiah 60. Something amazing is prophesied here. The glory of God is so present with us that it changes everything. Gentiles will be drawn to this glory seen on us. Kings will come to the brightness. The wealth of the nations will come to the people of God because of this visible glory. I am not making this up. The text is quite clear.

Araphel

Now we come to the remarkable hidden clue to understanding this passage. It is found in verse two. The word *darkness* appears twice in English translations. If that is the correct translation, then darkness covers everyone. However, I challenge you to consider a better translation. In the Hebrew text, two completely different and opposite words are translated as *darkness.*

The first time, the word is *choshek.* It means just what we think. It means evil darkness. But the second word translated darkness, is *araphel.* (Note: the adjective *deep or gross* is not in the Hebrew.) Araphel has a different usage. Unfortunately, it is normally translated as darkness, but it only occurs ten times prior to Isaiah 60 in the Old Testament. It is not difficult to look at these earlier verses and draw a clear conclusion from the contextual comparisons. My conclusion is this. *Araphel* does not mean evil darkness, but rather it means the cloud of glory around God, the mist of God. It is a protection for those inside this *araphel*.

The throne of God and the place where Jesus lives in Heaven is described this way:

> *Who alone has immortality, dwelling in* **unapproachable light,** *whom no man has seen or can see, to whom be honor and everlasting power. Amen* (1 Timothy 6:16).

Contrast this verse with the idea that is conveyed in the following verses. Then consider what those verses would sound like if you said *glory cloud* instead.

> Exodus 20:21 *So the people stood afar off, but Moses drew near the thick darkness (glory cloud: araphel) where God was.*

> Deuteronomy 4:11 *Then you came near and stood at the foot of the mountain, and the mountain burned with fire to the midst of heaven, with darkness (choshek), cloud, and thick darkness (glory cloud: araphel).*

> Deuteronomy 5:22 *These words Yahweh spoke to all your assembly, in the mountain from the midst of the fire, the cloud, and the thick darkness (glory cloud: araphel), with a loud voice; and He added no more. And He wrote them on two tablets of stone and gave them to me.*

2 Samuel 22:10 He bowed the heavens also, and came down with darkness (glory cloud: araphel) under His feet.

1 Kings 8:12 & 2 Chron. 6:1 (same verse) *Then Solomon spoke: Yahweh said He would dwell in the dark cloud (glory cloud: araphel).*

Job 22:13 *And you say, 'What does God know? Can He judge through the deep darkness (glory cloud: araphel)?'*

Job 38:9 *When I made the clouds its garment, And thick darkness (glory cloud: araphel) its swaddling band;*

Psalm 18:9 *He bowed the heavens also, and came down with darkness (glory cloud: araphel) under His feet.*

Psalm 97:2 *Clouds and darkness (glory cloud: araphel) surround Him; Righteousness and justice are the foundation of His throne.*

These ten verses are the only ones in the Bible before Isaiah 60 that use *araphel*. I ask you. If we stipulate that God's dwelling is in *unapproachable light,* then how can they translate *araphel* as darkness every time? I submit to you that this is a mistaken translation and that *araphel,* instead, speaks of the glory cloud, the mist of God, the glorious shield of Yahweh! Each of the above verses makes much more sense when thinking of *araphel* as a cloud of mist or fog of God's glory.

Take just the last one, Psalm 97:2. If you think of the darkness that surrounds YAHWEH as evil darkness, it contradicts everything else the Bible says about God. On the other hand, if you say He is surrounded by a glory cloud it is then consistent with the nature of God.

Now, let's go back to Isaiah 60:2. Try it with my suggested translation:

darkness (evil darkness, choshek) *shall cover the earth, And deep darkness* (araphel, the glory cloud or mist of God) *the people;*

That makes much more sense. To paraphrase: *at a time when darkness covers the earth, My glory cloud will cover My people.* Rather than see this verse as a Hebrew parallelism, I see it as contrasting two extremes and declaring protection for His people. (Note: the word for *people* here is consistent with my interpretation).

The Last Generation

We began this book with proof from Psalm 102 that we are now in the *generation last*. I believe Isaiah 60 is also to be uniquely applied to the final generation of this age. As wickedness and violence increase, God is doing something marvelous in His people. Through restoration and mercy toward Israel, He is preparing for the grand reconciliation of one new man in Christ Jesus. This is not only for our comfort, but it make us ready to stand for Him against all odds. We will indeed pass through the valley of the shadow of death, and there will certainly be martyrs. Yet, He will prepare a table for us *in the presence* of our enemies. There will be an unprecedented impartation of the glory of YAHWEH placed on His people. We will be as Daniel prophesied.

> *Those who do wickedly against the covenant he shall corrupt with flattery; but the people who know their God shall be strong, and carry out great exploits* (Daniel 11:32).

Some may accuse me of spreading doom and gloom, but I see it rather, as gloom and va-voom! As I started this chapter, people ask if it will get better and better, or worse and worse, until Jesus comes. The answer is still yes. It will get better for believers, and worse for the ungodly.

> *Blow the trumpet in Zion, And sound an alarm in My holy mountain! Let all the inhabitants of the land tremble; For the day of the LORD (YAHWEH) is coming, For it is at hand: A day of* **darkness** *and gloominess, A day of clouds and* **thick darkness (glory cloud: araphel)** (Joel 2:1-1).

Using our new understanding of *araphel*, the above verse says the day of the LORD will be both: *choshek*, evil darkness and *araphel*, the mist or the glory of God.

With all the evil darkness that is coming on the earth, it is imperative that we wake up, put on our armor, fill our lamps with the oil of the Holy Spirit, embrace the glory, and stand for God. Stand for His Kingdom. Stand for His King. It is time. The fight is on. I never tire of the old cliché: I've read the end of the Book, and we win!

> *Then I heard a loud voice saying in heaven, Now salvation, and strength, and the kingdom of our God, and the power of His Christ have come, for the accuser of our brethren, who accused them before our God day and night, has been cast down.* **And they overcame him** *by the blood of the Lamb and by the word of their testimony, and they did not love their lives to the death* (Revelation 12:10-11).

YAHWEH, GOD OF CREATION, IS FAITHFUL!